Cuba Constitución

The new Constitutional Laws for Cuba

Text of the Recent Measures for the Self-Government of the Island

Cuba Constitución

The new Constitutional Laws for Cuba
Text of the Recent Measures for the Self-Government of the Island

ISBN/EAN: 9783744728850

Printed in Europe, USA, Canada, Australia, Japan

Cover: Foto ©Suzi / pixelio.de

More available books at **www.hansebooks.com**

THE NEW
CONSTITUTIONAL LAWS
FOR CUBA.

TEXT OF THE RECENT MEASURES FOR THE
SELF-GOVERNMENT OF THE ISLAND,
WITH COMMENTS THEREON.

ALSO A BRIEF REVIEW OF THE EVOLUTION OF SPANISH COLONIZATION, AND A STATISTICAL COMPARISON OF THE PROGRESS OF CUBA UNDER SPANISH RULE WITH THAT OF INDEPENDENT SPANISH-AMERICAN COUNTRIES.

NEW YORK:
PUBLISHED BY THE ASSOCIATED SPANISH AND CUBAN PRESS,
Bowling Green Building, 11 Broadway.
1897.

BLUMENBERG
PRESS
NEW
YORK

TO HIS EXCELLENCY

DON ENRIQUE DUPUY DE LOME,

SPANISH MINISTER IN WASHINGTON,

WHO HAS WITH SUCH DIPLOMATIC SKILL PROMOTED THE FRIENDLY AND HONORABLE RELATIONS BETWEEN SPAIN AND THE UNITED STATES, WHILE UPHOLDING WITH PATRIOTIC ZEAL AND EFFICIENCY THE INALIENABLE RIGHTS OF SPAIN IN AMERICA,

THIS WORK IS RESPECTFULLY DEDICATED.

CONTENTS.

PART FIRST.

Methods of Early Spanish Colonization.—Evolution of the Modern Colonial Polity of Spain.—The Latest Measure of Home Rule Granted to Cuba and Porto Rico Compared with the Political System in Other Foreign Colonies.

By ARTURO CUYÁS.

PART SECOND.

Expository Preamble and Royal Decree Sanctioning the Plan for the Extension in Scope of the Abarzuza Reform Law of 1895. – Commentary: Expressions of Opinion by Party Leaders and the Press.—Text of the Abarzuza Law.

By ANTONIO CUYÁS.

PART THIRD.

Political and Social Condition of the Island of Cuba.—Statistics of Its Wealth and Commercial Movement.—Its Progress Under Spanish Rule Compared with That of Independent Spanish-American Countries.

By L. V. ABAD DE LAS CASAS.

Part First.

I. Methods of Early Spanish Colonization.

II. Evolution of the Modern Colonial Policy of Spain.

III. The Latest Measure of Home Rule Granted to Cuba and Porto Rico Compared with the Political System in Other Foreign Colonies.

By Arturo Cuyás.

I.

METHODS OF EARLY SPANISH COLONIZATION.

Spain as Discoverer and Colonizer.

In the history of nations Spain stands foremost as the discoverer, conquerer and colonizer of new lands.

By the discovery of a new world, and the subjection of numberless tribes the Crown of Castile found itself toward the middle of the sixteenth century the undisputed possessor of such a vast domain as never before nor since came under the sway of a single nation.

Whatever may be said of the men who, moved principally by the restless spirit of adventure which was the dominant characteristic of that period, discovered and conquered the New World, the paternal solicitude and care of the Crown and its Councilors for the welfare of the subjugated Indians were made evident by wise laws, which stand as a monument of early civilization in America.

An eminent Cuban Autonomist, Señor Rafael M. Labra, for many years a Representative from Cuba in the Spanish Cortes, in his critical "History of Colonization," to which I shall have occasion to refer again, frankly admits that "by framing the famous Laws of the Indies, Spain justly laid claim to an enduring civilization, and to the foremost place among the great colonizing nations of modern times."*

English Historians Unjust to Spain.

English historians have never been willing to give Spain the credit due her for her early efforts in spreading Christianity and civilization among the savage tribes of the New World. On the contrary, race prejudice and the chagrin caused by Spain's achievements and her aggran-

* Labra, "La Colonización en la Historia," Vol. I., p. 47.

dizement in that epoch, and possibly also the contrast of the humane and paternal methods adopted by Spain with the policy of extermination which characterized the British treatment of the Indians, have made English historians virulent and bitter and notoriously unjust in their criticism of Spanish colonization.

A contributor to the *Irish World* has justly remarked in a recent issue of that paper:

Calumnies Handed Down.

"John Mitchell has said, in the preface to one of his historical works, that the greatest conquest England ever made was to gain the ear of the world. And so true is this that even we, Irish and Irish-Americans, knowing as we do her falseness and her craft, accept as gospel truth the calumnies handed down from one generation to another of English historians, and repeated by Anglo-American historians, of England's hereditary enemy—Spain."*

To such calumnies must be ascribed the false views prevailing in the United States in regard to Spain, its history, its laws, its customs and its manners.

The New School of American History.

Fortunately, a dispassionate observer, a scholar and historian, A. F. Bandelier, a pupil of the great Humboldt, has founded in this country a new school for the study of American history and for historical research; and one of the results of the well directed labors of that school has been the publication in Chicago of a most interesting, fascinating and truthful book by Chas. F. Lummis, entitled "The Spanish Pioneers."

In the preface of this book the following sentences occur: "That we have not given justice to the Spanish pioneers is simply because we have been misled. They made a record unparalleled; but our text books have not recognized that fact, though they no longer dare dispute it. Now, thanks to the new school of American history, we are coming to the truth—a truth which every manly

---

* M. S. in the *Irish World*, March 13, 1897.

American will be glad to know. We love manhood, and the Spanish pioneering of the Americas was the largest and longest and most marvelous feat of manhood in all history. It was not possible for a Saxon boy to learn that truth in my boyhood; it is enormously difficult, if possible, now."

Manhood of the Spanish Pioneers.

And so with the record of Spanish colonization and civilization of the New World. To quote again from the same author:

"When you know that the greatest of English text books has not even the name of the man who first sailed around the world (a Spaniard), nor of the man who discovered Brazil (a Spaniard), nor of him who discovered California (a Spaniard), nor of those Spaniards who first found and colonized in what is now the United States, and that it has a hundred other omissions as glaring and a hundred histories as untrue as the omissions are inexcusable, you will understand that it is high time we should do better justice than did our fathers to a subject which should be of the first interest to all real Americans.

Spaniards the First Civilizers.

"The Spanish were not only the first conquerers of the New World and its first colonizers, but also its first civilizers. They built the first cities, opened the first churches, schools and universities; brought the first printing presses, made the first books, wrote the first dictionaries, histories and geographies, and brought the first missionaries; and before New England had a real newspaper Mexico had a seventeenth century attempt at one!

"One of the wonderful things about this Spanish pioneering—almost as remarkable as the pioneering itself—was the humane and progressive spirit which marked it from first to last. Histories of the sort long current speak of that hero nation as cruel to the Indians; but in truth the record of Spain in that respect puts us to the blush. The legislation of Spain in behalf of the Indians everywhere was incomparably more extensive, more comprehensive,

Humane and Progressive Spirit of Spanish Pioneers.

more systematic and more humane than that of Great Britain, the Colonies and the present United States all combined. Those first teachers gave the Spanish language and Christian faith to a thousand aborigines where we gave a new language and religion to one. There have been Spanish schools for Indians in America since 1524. By 1575—nearly a century before there was a printing press in English America—many books in *twelve* different Indian languages had been printed in the City of Mexico, whereas in our history John Eliot's Indian Bible stands alone; and three Spanish universities in America were nearly rounding out their century when Harvard was founded. A surprisingly large proportion of the pioneers of America were college men; and intelligence went hand in hand with heroism in the early settlement of the New World."*

Spain Not Responsible for Individual Misdeeds.

No attempt shall be made here to excuse, palliate or condone the heinous deeds of some of the men who first set foot in America. Taken by themselves they should be strongly condemned; but such individual misdeeds should not be imputed to the whole Spanish nation, nor be made the only salient feature of early Spanish colonization.

It should be remembered that "it was in the very year of the discovery of America that the Spaniards, in the conquest of Granada, had finished their eight centuries of continuous war for wresting their proud country from the invading Moors. This war had made every Spaniard a fighter and every infidel an enemy exempted from all tolerance and mercy." **

As the well equipped historian Prescott says in his preface to the "History of the Conquest of Mexico": "The distance of the present age from the period of the narrative might be presumed to secure the historian from undue

* "The Spanish Pioneers," p. 23.

** George Edward Ellis in "Narrative and Critical History of America," Vol. II., p. 301.

prejudice or partiality. Yet, to American and English readers, acknowledging so different a moral standard from that of the sixteenth century, I may possibly be thought too indulgent to the errors of the conquerors. To such I can only say that while, on the one hand, I have not hesitated to expose in their strongest colors the excesses of the conquerors, on the other, I have given them the benefit of such mitigating reflections as might be suggested by the circumstances and the period in which they lived."

Circumstances and Period Should Be Borne in Mind.

We must bear in mind that "what are considered now as self-evident truths about universal rights were far enough from being self-evident in the sixteenth century. On the contrary, they were extremely unfamiliar and abstruse conceptions, toward which the most enlightened minds could only grope their way by slow degrees."*

Perpetrators of Horrors Behaved as Ruffians, Not as Spaniards.

"We must take care not to identify too indiscriminately the Spaniards, as such, with the horrors perpetrated in Hispaniola. It was not in the character of Spaniards so much as in the character of ruffians that the perpetrators behaved, and there have been ruffians enough among people who speak English."**

"A great deal of sentimental ink has been shed over the wickedness of the Spaniards in crossing the ocean and attacking people who had never done them any harm, overturning and obliterating a 'splendid civilization,' and more to the same effect. * * * Yet, if we are to be guided by strict logic, it would be difficult to condemn the Spaniards for the mere act of conquering Mexico without involving in the same condemnation our own forefathers, who crossed the ocean and overran the territory of the United States, with small regard for the proprietary rights of Algonquins or Iroquois, or red men of any sort. Our forefathers, if called upon to justify themselves, would have replied that they were founding Christian States and dif-

* John Fiske, "The Discovery of America," Vol. II., p. 456.
** Ibid, Vol. II., p. 443.

fusing the blessings of a higher civilization. Now, if we would not lose or distort the historical perspective, we must bear in mind that the Spanish conquerors would have returned exactly the same answer."*

Redeeming Features of Spanish Colonization.

It is precisely in "founding Christian states and diffusing the blessings of a higher civilization" among the Indians that we find the great redeeming features of Spanish colonization. As Señor Labra points out, "the colonizing efforts of Las Casas in Central America, of Irala in Paraguay, and of Vasco Nuñez in Darien were all inspired by a profound sympathy for the Indians, by a marked preference for peaceful means, the success of which was fully demonstrated, as well as by the purpose of harmonizing the existence of the Spaniards and the aborigines, causing the latter to enter by degrees into the enjoyment of the advantages and conveniences of the former."**

Sublime Work of Father Las Casas.

The contemplation of the lifelong and sublime work of Father Las Casas draws from the historian and philosopher, John Fiske, this glowing tribute: "In contemplating such a life as that of Las Casas, all words of eulogy seem weak and frivolous. The historian can only bow in reverent awe before a figure which is in some respects the most beautiful and sublime in the annals of Christianity since the apostolic age. When now and then, in the course of the centuries, God's providence brings such a life into this world, the memory of it must be cherished by mankind as one of its most precious and sacred possessions. For the thoughts, the words, the deeds of such a man there is no death. The sphere of their influence goes on widening forever. They bud, they blossom, they bear fruit from age to age."***

Were it my purpose to contrast here the Spanish policy of early colonization with the methods employed by Por-

* John Fiske, "The Discovery of America," Vol. II., p. 291.

** Labra, "La Colonización en la Historia," Vol. II., p. 98.

*** John Fiske, "The Discovery of America," Vol. II., p. 482.

tuguese, Dutch, French and British colonizers, abundant material could be found in history to prove that "Spain cannot be denied the foremost place among colonizing nations."* While Spain's principal aim was to teach religion and good morals to the subjugated Indians, raising them to the level of the conquerors, Portugal, Holland and Great Britain for a long time considered their colonies only as profitable markets and treated the natives as slaves. Señor Labra, the Cuban Autonomist, devotes two entire chapters of the work above cited to a comparison such as has been indicated, demonstrating with numerous quotations the wise and humane spirit of the Laws of the Indies, the compilation of which was begun in 1570 by Philip II. and concluded in 1660; and this impartial Cuban, who is an authority on the history and exposition of law, indignantly refutes the opinions unfavorable to Spanish colonization advanced by such historians as Robertson and Roscher.**

Contrast with the Methods of Other Colonizers.

Long after Spain, under Charles V., had decreed the freedom of the Indians and made them subjects of Spain, with the same rights as the Spanish born, the British introduced white slaves into America, who, as "indented" and "convict" servants, were sold at £40 or £50 per head. The Dutch were the first to introduce the African slave trade into America (in 1620)—according to Bancroft —a curse which the British extended later on to the West Indies.

British and Dutch Imported White and Colored Slaves into America.

And as for financial oppression, never were the subjects of Spain in the New World so heavily and so unjustly taxed as were the British colonists by the Navigation Acts, the creation of the Oriental Companies, the bill of 1699 against woolens, and other oppressive measures. Nay, the Declaration of Independence of the thirteen colonies

Financial Oppression of British Colonists.

---

* Labra, "La Colonización en la Historia," Vol. II., p. 84.

** Ibid, Vol. II., Chap. 13, p. 83, and Chap. 14, p. 113.

of North America, with its list of grievances, stands an everlasting monument to the grasping, deaf and blind cupidity of Great Britain.

Moral and Material Progress of British and Spanish Colonists Contrasted.

As regards progress, there is nothing on this continent to show that Great Britain, up to the time of the American Revolution, had done anything to ameliorate the condition of the colonists. On the other hand, Mexico and the other Spanish-American republics can boast of numerous public works left by the Spanish; beautiful cities,* magnificent churches and cathedrals, fine universities, colleges and hospitals, several mints, various aqueducts and viaducts, interesting museums, palatial residences, artistic monuments and innumerable mines, all built and equipped under Spanish rule centuries before the American colonies revolted against the tyranny of the British Government.

While the policy of Great Britain toward the aboriginal tribes of North America had been one of spoliation and merciless extermination, the policy of Spain, as is clearly stated in the ordinance issued by Charles V. in 1526, consisted in "teaching the Indians good morals, leading them away from vice and cannibalism, preaching the Gospel to them and instructing them in the doctrine of our Catholic faith for the salvation of their souls, and bringing them under our sovereignty, so that they may be treated, favored and protected the same as all our other subjects and vassals."**

Thus, while the aboriginal inhabitants of North America have well nigh disappeared under the aggressive extension of Anglo-Saxon occupation, the Indians of Spanish America, under "the most complete and comprehensive scheme of Colonial Government which the world has ever

---

* Baron von Humboldt, speaking of the capital of Mexico, said it was "the city of palaces, and the handsomest capital in America."

** "Recopilación de Indias," Book I., title 1, section 3.

known,"* have subsisted and become civilized: "They have been saved and educated to be citizens all, and among them important scholars, great engineers and sometime presidents of a republic."**

Moral and Material Progress of British and Spanish Colonists Contrasted.

"The Spaniard never robbed the brown first Americans of their homes, nor drove them on and on before him; on the contrary, he protected and secured to them by special laws the undisturbed possession of their lands for all time. It is due to the generous and manly laws made by Spain three hundred years ago, that our most interesting and advanced Indians, the Pueblos, enjoy to-day full security in their lands, while nearly all others (who never came fully under Spanish dominion) have been time after time ousted from lands our Government had solemnly given to them."***

"In the United States the aborigines are represented in a very small measure, and the tribes which have not been massacred live still in a semi-savage condition on reservations, more or less respected. On the other hand, in Spanish America the bulk of the population is composed of Spaniolized Indians, who, while receiving the European civilization and mixing with the races from the Old World, are not the less representatives of the original American race."****

Herein lies the contrast between the two systems of colonization: while "Neo-Saxons have destroyed or driven out the native population, Neo-Latins have assimilated them."***** The work of assimilation, regulated by wise

* S. T. Wallis, "Spain, Her Institutions and Public Men," p. 70.

** "The Awakening of a Nation," by Chas. F. Lummis, *Harper's Magazine*, March, 1897.

*** Chas. F. Lummis, "The Spanish Pioneers," p. 149.

**** Réclus, "Geographie Universelle," Vol. XVII., p. 14.

***** Antony Meray, "Aptitudes of Human Races," *Revue Moderne*, September, 1857.

laws, began almost as soon as the rulers of Spain were made aware of the vast discoveries and conquests in the New World.

Wisdom and Humanity of Spanish Laws for the Indians.

"Although no doubt greatly defective in many particulars, and tinctured most prejudicially with the errors in political economy which were peculiar to the times, the Recopilación de Indias (Laws of the Indies) bears all about it evidences of the most far-seeing wisdom, the most laborious and comprehensive investigation and management of details, and a spirit of enlightened humanity not easily to be exceeded." *

I will close these introductory remarks showing the spirit of Spanish colonization with another quotation from "The Spanish Pioneers." Speaking of Pizarro, Mr. Lummis says: "Indeed, he was carrying out with great success that general Spanish principle that the chief wealth of a country is not its gold or its timber or its lands, but its *people*. It was everywhere the attempt of the Spanish pioneers to uplift and Christianize and civilize the savage inhabitants, so as to make them worthy citizens of the new nation, instead of wiping them off the face of the earth to make room for the newcomers, as has been the general fashion of some European conquests. Now and then there were mistakes and crimes by individuals; but the great principle of wisdom and humanity marks the whole broad course of Spain—a course which challenges the admiration of every manly man."**

* S. T. Wallis, "Spain," p. 70.

** Lummis, "The Spanish Pioneers," p. 276.

II.

EVOLUTION OF THE MODERN COLONIAL POLITY OF SPAIN.

Traditional Policy of Spain Toward American Colonies.

The object of the foregoing brief retrospective view is to show what has been the traditional policy of Spain toward her American colonies ever since the discovery of the New World.

There may have been men—Viceroys and Governors—who have abused the power given them by Spain to administer her laws in what was called the Indies; but to the Spanish Monarchs and the men who ruled the destinies of Spain the credit is due of having had lofty ideals and of having been guided by wise counsel in framing the laws which were to govern their subjects across the seas.

In this respect Cuba and Porto Rico have had little cause to complain, for the Spanish Government has been ever mindful of the interests of the two islands, and has gradually—perhaps slowly at times—but surely, granted nearly all the liberties, reforms and concessions demanded by their inhabitants.

Systematic Attacks of Cuban Malcontents.

There are in all countries refractory people, impatient grumblers and malcontents, who systematically attack their own Government for not following the radical policy which they themselves would dictate.

Of such men as these George Washington has said: "Against the malignity of the discontented, the turbulent and vicious, no abilities, no exertions, nor the most unshaken integrity are a safeguard."

Such has been the case with the Cuban agitators. Had they devoted their efforts and their energies to obtaining from the mother country by peaceful and legal means the liberties they have sought through revolutionary methods, they would not have hindered nor retarded the process of evolution, nor brought that beautiful and once prosperous Island to the verge of ruin and desolation.

Political Evolution in Cuba and Porto Rico Has Kept Pace with That of Spain.

The introduction of liberal reforms in the Spanish West Indies has not been as rapid as some people with radical views might wish, but these reforms certainly have kept pace with the political evolution of Spain.

The period of peace which has enabled Spain to make rapid strides on the road of progress and attain a prosperity which is hardly known abroad, dates from the middle of the present century. Until then the spirit of revolt and brigandage was rampant in the Peninsula, due, in no small measure, to the guerilla warfare which the people had to adopt in order to get rid of the French invaders. The country had hardly regained its independence, at the beginning of this century, when the adoption of a more liberal system of government, substituting the representative form for an absolute monarchy, caused great strife and internecine wars.

During that period of turmoil, when the institutions of Spain were undergoing such a radical change, its Government could ill afford to implant in the far-away colonies any political reforms which had not yet been tried in the mother country. It was only after peace had been completely restored at home that, one by one, all the political innovations and democratic institutions of modern times were gradually adopted in Spain, until it stands to-day, as has been acknowledged even by such a staunch republican as Señor Castelar, among the freest nations of the earth.

First Constitutional Privileges and Representation in the Cortes Extended to the Colonies.

And yet, in the midst of the upheaval which the ancient political institutions of Spain were undergoing in the first half of this century, twice were the newly adopted Constitutions of Spain and representation in the Spanish Cortes extended to the colonies; besides which reforms were granted to them that were considered very liberal at that time, including the creation of Boards of Aldermen and Provincial Assemblies.

Other Liberal Measures Introduced.

Several liberal measures (such as the abolition of the Royal monopoly of the manufacture of tobacco in 1817, and the freedom of commercial intercourse at all ports of Cuba in 1818) were granted to the Island at the solicitation of the eminent Cuban patriot, Francisco Arango. From that time on several other laws were passed tending to improve the condition of the colonies, and owing to these, to the stream of immigration from Spain, and to the exemption from military service which permitted the inhabitants of Cuba to devote all their energies to agricultural and industrial pursuits, while a detachment of the Spanish army garrisoned the ports to prevent a repetition of any attacks from abroad, soon the Island of Cuba began to develop wondrous wealth.

Two factors contributed principally to the enormous growth of the production and commerce of the Island: the slave trade, which had been introduced in Cuba by the English during their occupation of Havana in 1762–63, and the influx of Spanish merchants and agriculturists, who left the Spanish possessions on the continent when the latter rebelled against Spain and went to settle in Cuba. To the combined efforts of those two elements, negro hands in the fields and Spanish capital, brains and activity, the Island owed its steady development, until its revenue reached in 1861 a total of $26,423,228 against $1,500,000 in 1782, and only $824,612 in 1791, after the second war with England.

Free Titles to Land Belonging to the Crown Given to Settlers.

A great part of the land of Cuba belonging to the Crown was parceled out, and free titles given to a number of settlers, a gift unparalleled in the history of monarchical countries. From 1811 to 1814, and from 1820 to 1823, were two periods of constitutional monarchy in Spain, and the provisions of both liberal Constitutions were extended to Cuba.

A dispassionate historian, Pezuela, writing on Cuba in

Special System of Government Enabled Cuba to Develop Resources and Wealth.

1863, says: "In 1836 the Peninsula settled into a constitutional form of government, and the reason why its Constitution was not immediately applied to Cuba is to be found in the great evils which former experiments brought to the Island, as is demonstrated and evidenced by many facts. Since then the Island has been governed by a special system which, although not devoid of defects, which time and experience, however, will gradually correct, has enabled the Island to develop its resources and wealth to such a degree as to admit of a favorable comparison with the progress attained in the same period by countries which claim more liberal forms of government."*

This opinion is confirmed by Señor Labra, when he says, comparing the methods of colonization of different European countries in the far East, up to 1868, "The least violent, the least oppressive, the most imbued with a progressive spirit, were those pursued by Spain."**

First Steps Toward Abolishing Slavery.

During the war of secession in the United States there was a period of expectancy, the abolition of slavery being a problem in the solution of which Cuba was particularly interested. No sooner had it been settled and peace restored in the United States than the Spanish Government considered the time ripe for introducing some reforms in Cuba, and with this end in view a consulting committee composed of many prominent Cubans was called to Madrid in 1867, to confer with the Government and present the views of the Cuban people.

Unfortunately, before a plan could be agreed upon and adopted, Spain was convulsed once more by a democratic revolution, which drove the Queen from the throne and brought about a series of radical changes in the institutions of the country. Almost simultaneously with that revolution, in 1868, the uprising of the secessionist party in

*"Diccionario Geográfico, Estadístico, Histórico de la Isla de Cuba," by Jacobo de la Pezuela.

**"La Colonización en la Historia," Vol. II., p. 365.

Cuba took place, adding to Spain's local troubles a rebellion in her distant colony, which lasted nearly ten years.

First Insurrection In Cuba Retarded Liberal Progress.

It was out of the question to establish political reforms in Cuba while the insurrection was going on; but as soon as the Island was pacified a series of liberal measures were gradually granted, which more than fulfilled all the conditions set forth in the articles of capitulation submitted by the rebels in arms and accepted by Spain previous to their surrender in 1878.

Notwithstanding all that has been said as to Spain not keeping faith with the insurgents, it is a positive fact, well sustained by undeniable evidence in the shape of laws which now govern the Island of Cuba, that the Government of Spain has granted much more than the insurgents demanded in their covenant, called the Treaty of Zanjón.

Spain Conceded to Rebels More Than They Asked by Treaty of Zanjon.

In the articles of capitulation nothing was said about representation in the Cortes, nor about the total abolition of slavery, nor about extending to Cuba the Constitution of Spain; and yet all these concessions have been granted.

According to the articles of capitulation the insurgents were satisfied to have for Cuba the same politic, organic and administrative laws then in force in Porto Rico; and a comparison of the laws now governing Cuba with those governing Porto Rico at that time will clearly demonstrate that the Cubans have received more than the insurgents asked for.

The articles of capitulation demanded free pardon and amnesty to all rebels and deserters, and freedom for the coolies and the slaves who were in the insurgent ranks. Spain granted amnesty and free pardon to all offenders, and by a very wise law, framed by Señor Moret, provided for the total abolition of slavery in a gradual way, so as not to conflict by a too sudden change with existing conditions. Thus slavery has been totally abolished in Cuba without bloodshed and without injury to the interests of planters or to agriculture.

Several other measures extending to Cubans the same rights and liberties that Spaniards enjoy in Spain have been adopted by the Cortes and the Government.

New Constitution of Spain Proclaimed in Cuba in 1881.

In 1881 the Liberal Constitution of Spain of 1876 was proclaimed in Cuba. From that date the inhabitants of Cuba have enjoyed all the civil and political rights of Spanish subjects.

Under the Constitution no inhabitant of Cuba may be arrested except in the cases and in the manner prescribed by law. Within twenty-four hours of the arrest the prisoner must be discharged or surrendered to the judicial authorities; thereupon a judge having jurisdiction must, within seventy-two hours, either order the discharge of the prisoner or order his commitment to jail. Within the same limit of time the prisoner must be informed of the decision in his case. (Art. IV. of the Constitution.)

No Spaniard, and consequently no Cuban, may be committed except upon the warrant of a judge having jurisdiction. Within seventy-two hours of the commitment the prisoner must be granted a hearing and the warrant of commitment either sustained or quashed. (Art. V.)

Any person arrested or committed without the formalities required by law, unless his case fall within the exceptions made by the Constitution and by the laws, shall be discharged upon his own petition, or upon the petition of any Spanish subject. (Art. V.)

No one shall enter the dwelling of a Cuban without his consent except in the cases and in the manner prescribed by law. (Art. VI.)

His mail while in charge of the Post Office shall neither be opened nor withheld. (Art. VII.)

He shall not be compelled to change his dwelling or residence except upon the order of an authority competent thereto and in the cases provided by law. (Art. IX.)

The penalty of confiscation of property shall never be imposed upon him; nor may he be deprived of his private property unless by due process of law, and, when the expropriation be for public use, after a previous just compensation. If there be no previous just compensation the courts shall protect his rights, and in the proper case restore him to the possession of his property. (Art. X.)

Constitutional Rights and Guarantees.

The Roman Catholic and Apostolic religion is the religion of the State. But no Cuban shall suffer molestation on account of his religious opinions, nor be disturbed in the practice of his faith, provided he duly respect Christian morals. (Art. XI.)

The learned professions are open to all Spanish subjects and they may obtain their professional instruction in any manner they deem fit. Any Spanish subject may establish and conduct a school, in accordance with the laws. (Art. XII.)

Every Cuban, like every Spaniard, has the right:

Freely to express his ideas and opinions, orally or in writing, using the printing press or any similar device, without censorship.

Peaceably to assemble.

To form associations.

To petition, by himself or in combination with others, the King, the Cortes and the authorities.

The right to petition is denied only to armed forces. (Art. XIII.)

All Cubans are eligible to public office, according to their merit and capacity. (Art. XV.)

The constitutional rights conceded to Cubans are guaranteed by the provisions of laws passed to enforce the Constitution. These laws provide remedies, civil and criminal, for the infringement of constitutional rights by judges, authorities and functionaries of all classes. (Art. XVI.)

All these constitutional rights of the inhabitants of Cuba, which render their citizenship as valuable a protec-

Representation of Cuba and Porto Rico in the Spanish Cortes.

tion as the citizenship of any other state, no matter how democratic, were secured by the organization of municipalities and provincial assemblies, and above all by representation in the Cortes, as provided by the two following articles of the Constitution:

ART. 89. The colonial provinces shall be governed by special laws; but the Government is authorized to extend to these provinces the laws proclaimed or that may be proclaimed for the Peninsula, with the modifications it may deem proper, informing the Cortes thereof.

Cuba and Porto Rico shall be represented in the Cortes of the Kingdom in the manner that shall be prescribed by a special law, and this law may differ for each of the islands.

PROVISIONAL ARTICLE. The Government shall determine when and in what manner the representatives of the Island of Cuba to the Cortes shall be elected.

Cubans have therefore the following constitutional rights firmly established by the organic law: Personal security against arbitrary arrest; inviolability of the domicile; security of the secrecy of correspondence; security against confiscation of property; the suffrage; freedom of worship; freedom of education, and freedom of the study and practice of professions; freedom of speech; freedom of the press; right of peaceable assembly; right to form associations; right to petition; eligibility to all public offices, and a muncipal and provincial government.

Is it therefore reasonable to speak of the "despotism of the mother country," or of the "irritating condition of the Island of Cuba" ?*

To the oft-repeated assertion that the Cubans are taxed without having representation in the Cortes, the only reply that need be made is that ever since 1878 Cuba has had representation in the Spanish Cortes; that her representatives have a voice, not only as regards the affairs of Cuba, but also in the shaping of all national affairs, a privilege never enjoyed by any colonist of Great Britain; that in 1892 a new electoral law was passed extending the right

* "Spanish Rule in Cuba: Laws Governing the Island," p. 20.

of suffrage to all persons paying taxes to the amount of $5 or having a professional diploma or academic degree; that Cuba, with a population of 1,600,000, sends thirteen Senators and thirty Representatives to the Spanish Cortes, while the State of New York, with 6,513,000 inhabitants, sends only two Senators and thirty-four Representatives to Congress. Thus it will be seen that Cubans are well represented in the lawmaking bodies of the Spanish Government.

New Reforms Framed by Maura in 1893 and by Abarzuza in 1895.

But liberal as were these concessions, the statesmen of Spain were intent upon enlarging their scope by introducing new reforms in accordance with the spirit of the times. No later than 1893 Señor Maura, then Minister for the Colonies, framed a Reform Law which was much discussed in the Cortes, and which would have established in Cuba a new régime little short of autonomy. A change of ministry prevented that act from being passed, but subsequently Señor Abarzuza, a Cuban by birth, being appointed Minister for the Colonies, presented the same bill with a few slight modifications, and it was unanimously passed by both branches of the Cortes, the men of all parties joining in approval of a law which would have greatly benefited the inhabitants of Cuba.

Cuban Secessionists Revolt to Prevent Reforms Being Promulgated.

But the Cuban agitators in the United States prevented its promulgation in the Island by inducing a few secessionists there to join them in a revolt, which soon increased in magnitude, owing to the great number of negro laborers who were idle on account of a monetary crisis due to the low price of sugar. It has always been the purpose of Cuban secessionists to prevent any liberal measure being adopted in Cuba, as removing any just cause of complaint on which to base their rebellious attitude.

Though retarded by the insurrection which broke out in February, 1895, ten days after its passage, said Reform Law, with additional concessions which will amount practically to home rule, is about to be put in force in Cuba.

Promises Made by the Crown and Government Faithfully Carried Out.

Thus the promises of autonomic administration solemnly made by the Queen Regent in her last message to the Cortes, and subsequently confirmed on July 14 by the Prime Minister, Señor Canovas, in a memorable speech, when he declared that "the sincerity both of Her Majesty and the Government in promising more ample and liberal reforms for Cuba was unquestionable," will have been faithfully carried out.

Liberal Concessions of 1895 Considerably Broadened by Senor Canovas in 1897.

The liberal concessions embodied in the Abarzuza law of 1895 have been considerably broadened and enlarged by the Royal Decree of February 3, 1897, in the framing of which Señor Cánovas, the leader of the Conservative party, has shown a progressive spirit that has brought him unstinted praise, even from the leaders of the opposition. It is fair to assume that Cuba, having fared so well at the hands of the Conservative Government, has nothing to fear from the advent of the Liberals to power.

And we must come to the conclusion that those Cubans love their country best who, by dint of unceasing, albeit peaceful, efforts in the political field, of patient though persevering work in favor of autonomic ideals, have, stone by stone, paved the way for progressive home rule. To the blindness and folly of a few who have resorted to revolutionary methods and plunged the country into war the Island owes nothing but ruin, devastation and misery; the loss of prosperity and credit; the heavy burden of a war debt.

Cuban Agitators Responsible for Calamities.

And yet the Cuban agitators, who are responsible for all these calamities, and who have done more harm to Cuba in a few years than all the denounced misrule of Spain in centuries, accuse the Spanish Government of burdening Cuba with a heavy debt. The blame should be laid where it belongs. Cuba had no debt before the first rebellion broke out. "Porto Rico has never risen in revolt. It has no debt."*

*"Spanish Rule in Cuba: Laws Governing the Island," p. 41.

III.

THE LATEST MEASURE OF HOME RULE GRANTED TO CUBA AND PORTO RICO COMPARED WITH THE POLITICAL SYSTEM IN OTHER FOREIGN COLONIES.

Unlike British Colonists, Cubans and Porto Ricans Have a Representative Voice in the Supreme Government.

By the new reform measure framed by Señor Canovas, Cuba will enjoy a more liberal and advanced system of government than any other colony, except possibly a few British possessions favored with responsible government; yet in the latter natives are debarred from representation in the home Parliament, and from holding office in the home Government, while "the natives of Cuba and Porto Rico have free access to all official careers. They hold office, on equal terms with the natives of the Peninsula, in the civil administration, the judiciary, the army, the navy and the church. They have their share, without restriction, in the national life in all its aspects. Cubans and Porto Ricans, as representatives of their provinces in the Senate and in the Chamber of Deputies, take part in the legislation for the whole Spanish nation."*

This political privilege Great Britain has invariably denied to all her colonies. While the Latin countries, notably Spain, France and Portugal, have adopted a policy of assimilation, forming with their dependencies "a sort of confederation, whereby the colony has a representative voice in the supreme government,"** "the inhabitants of the United Kingdom have always been decidedly hostile to the admission of colonial representatives into the Houses of Parliament."*** In this respect "the Isle of Man and

*"Spanish Rule in Cuba: Laws Governing the Island," pp. 41, 46.

** Encyclopædia Britannica, Vol. XI., p. 20.

*** La Grande Encyclopædie.

the Channel Islands are as completely separated from England as New Zealand and Canada."*

Difference in Methods of Colonization Due to Racial Characteristics.

This is a characteristic trait of polity which must not be lost sight of in drawing a comparison between the respective régimes in British and Spanish possessions. In fact no comparison should be drawn without first taking into consideration the different—nay, opposite—traits of character of the Latin and Anglo-Saxon races, to which must principally be ascribed the difference in their methods of colonization.

Taking them at their origin we find that the Government of Spain bore the expense of the discovery and conquest, sent fleets and men across the seas, directing the efforts of pioneers, framed laws to regulate trade, adopted a system of colonization by creating municipalities, establishing parishes, endowing schools and hospitals, and took a deep interest in the growth and development of her new colonies, which was closely watched and directed from home.

England Took No Concern in the Birth and Growth of Her Colonies.

England, on the other hand, took no particular pains to encourage or uphold the efforts of British discoverers and colonizers. "Englishmen were mustering on the Atlantic coast of North America, organizing natural and simple Governments, and preparing for their march of 3,000 miles westward, and yet the Government and people of England were utterly ignorant that any such process was going on at all."** English colonists acted with entire independence of the mother country, for England, as well as Holland, simply protected individual enterprises by means of charters. Lechevalier, in his monumental work on colonial affairs, says: "While it is a fact that after the sixteenth century, and particularly after the end of the last century, England has seen her domain extend over all parts of the

* Encyclopædia Britannica.

** Ibid, Vol. XXIII., p. 731.

world, she had not yet a well-defined colonial polity. It is only the individual initiative of her subjects which has pushed her toward distant settlements; the instinct of her own good fortune has done the rest. The following line from Ovid can now be applied to her:

"Et quod nunc ratio est, impetus ante fuit."*

The Spanish Paternal Method in Colonial Government.

Thus in the Spanish paternal method of keeping the colonies closely bound to the metropolis we find reflected the racial characteristic of close family ties, whereas the individual love of independence, which is a salient trait of Anglo-Saxon peoples, has shaped after a different pattern the formation, growth and development of English-speaking colonies.

It might truly be said that the latter were born free and independent, as far as the administration of local affairs was concerned, since the allegiance they owed to England was spontaneously offered by the patriotic zeal of English settlers without any effort or diligence on the part of the home Government. The only care of the metropolis was to secure, regulate and increase her commerce and trade with her colonies, and all the bills and acts passed by Parliament which had any bearing on the colonies had this sole end in view. As for their interior organization and administration, the home Government never gave them a thought.

The American Revolution Caused by Unbearable Burdens.

But the burdens imposed upon the colonies by the parent government became so unbearable that thirteen colonies in North America revolted and threw off the yoke, and in others the murmurs were so loud that it became imperative to apply a remedy.

"Complaints of misgovernment were frequent and the necessity for some reform in colonial administration was obvious and unquestionable, though the sagacity of British

---

* "Rapport sur les Questions Coloniales," by Jules Lechevalier, p. 10.

statesmen was severely tried to find an adequate solution to this perplexing and difficult problem."*

Threatening Attitude of Canada in 1838.

When Canada assumed a threatening attitude, Sir Robert Peel, in an eloquent speech (January 16, 1838), said: "It has been alleged that the majority of the people of Canada are disaffected to the British Government, and that, therefore, they ought to be released from their allegiance. Is this great country prepared to say, on the first manifestation of any rebellious feeling, 'Separate from us and establish a government for yourselves,' instead of recalling them to their duty? I think not. The application of this principle is perfectly inadmissible. If it applies to distant possessions, it applies also to those which are nearest to this country, and even to integral parts of the empire."

Introduction of Responsible Government in Canada in 1841.

It was only after the insurrection of 1839 in Canada, which, by the way, "was put down in a terrible, a most terrible manner,"** that the British Government, under Lord Melbourne, saw the necessity of modifying its colonial policy at once, which it did by introducing a form of responsible government into Canada in 1841; but for several years "the system itself was imperfectly understood and mistakes were made on all sides in the application of this hitherto untried experiment in colonial government to the practical administration of local affairs."***

After the lapse of seven years, when the new régime had been thoroughly and successfully tried in Canada, it was introduced (1848) into the maritime provinces, and subsequently it was gradually extended, from 1855 to 1890, to the several Australian colonies and the Cape of Good Hope. The confederation of the Canadian provinces

---

* "Parliamentary Government in the British Colonies," by Alpheus Todd, p. 26.

** Labra, "La Colonización en la Historia," Vol. II., p. 364.

*** Grey, "History of Colonial Policy," Vol. I., p. 205.

was effected by the establishment of a Dominion under the provisions of the British North America Act of 1867.

The Colonial Policy of Great Britain Shaping Itself Only of Late.

It is only of late years, therefore, that the colonial policy of Great Britain has shaped itself into a well-defined system, and according to their government relations with the Crown the colonies are arranged under three heads:

(1) Crown colonies, in which the Crown has the entire control of legislation, while the administration is carried out by public officers under the control of the home Government. (2) Colonies possessing representative institutions and irresponsible government, in which the Crown has only a veto on legislation, but the home Government retains the control of public officers. (3) Colonies possessing representative institutions and responsible government, in which the Crown has only a veto on legislation and the home Government has no control over any officer except the Governor.

Responsible Government Introduced Only Where Anglo-Saxon Population Predominates.

The form of responsible government has only been introduced into the most important possessions of Great Britain, where the Anglo-Saxon population is in the majority, and it was "avowedly introduced into the colonies for the purpose of reproducing in them a system of local self-government akin to that which prevails in the mother country, and to relieve the colonies from imperial interference in their domestic or internal concerns. The advocates of colonial reform had long striven to obtain such a modification in the methods of colonial administration as would confer upon British subjects in the colonies similar rights of self-government to those enjoyed by their fellow-citizens at home. This boon it was the expressed desire of the Imperial Government to bestow, so far at least as was compatible with the allegiance due to the Crown.

"The new polity granted to the colonies was not intended, however, to effect a fundamental change in the principles of government, by substituting democratic for monarchical rule. It was designed to extend to distant parts of the empire the practical benefits of a parliamentary system similar to that which exists in the parent state, and thus to render political institutions in the colonies, as far as possible, 'the very image and transcript of those of Great Britain.'"*

Right to Interfere Retained by England.

With the exception of the Dominion of Canada, "the mother country, however, still retains the right to interfere—either by advice, remonstrance, or, if need be, by active measures of control—whenever the powers of self-government are attempted to be exercised by any colony in an unlawful, unconstitutional or oppressive manner." **

"The whole question of the relations of the imperial authority to the representative colonies is one of great difficulty and delicacy. It requires consummate prudence and statesmanship to reconcile the metropolitan supremacy with the worthy spirit of colonial independence. As a matter of abstract right the mother country has never parted with the claim of ultimate, supreme authority for the imperial legislature. If it did so, it would dissolve the imperial tie and convert the colonies into foreign and independent states." ***

Provincial Legislation in British Colonies Subject to Crown Control.

In the Dominion of Canada the Governor General, appointed by and representing the Crown, is vested with absolute responsibility as to the power of interfering with provincial legislation; but, nevertheless, "the acts of subordinate legislatures throughout the empire must be liable to the constitutional supervision and control of the Crown in the last resort. This is necessary, not only for the purpose of maintaining the ultimate authority of the supreme

---

* Alpheus Todd, "Parliamentary Government in the British Colonies," p. 625.

** Ibid, p. 29.

*** "Historicus" (Sir W. Vernon Harcourt), London *Times*, June 1, 1879.

power, but likewise for the purpose of insuring that no colonial or provincial legislation shall be exercised unlawfully, or to the prejudice of other parts of the empire."*

Responsible Government a Failure in British West Indies.

It is a noticeable fact, and one that especially invites attention in connection with the introduction of a new régime in Cuba and Porto Rico, that the form of 'responsible government' has not worked equally well in different colonies of Great Britain. In the British West Indies, which have many geographical, topographical, climatic and ethnographic points of similarity with the Spanish West Indies, "the attempt to establish local self-government has proved to be a failure. After a fruitless endeavor to work the system successfully it was abandoned, and a simpler and more effective method of administration resorted to. This was notably the case in regard to Jamaica, which for nearly two centuries had possessed a representative Constitution, and had been latterly intrusted with a responsible government. In 1866 the local Legislature, at the instance of Governor Eyre, unanimously agreed to abrogate all the existing machinery of legislation and to accept in lieu thereof any form of government that might be approved by the Crown. Accordingly, by an Imperial Act passed in the same year, a new Constitution was conferred upon the island, and subsequently declared, by order in Council of May 19, 1884, to consist of a legislative council composed of four *ex-officio* members, five members appointed by the Crown and nine elective members. Besides this chamber there is a privy council of eight members appointed by the Crown, together with the Colonial Secretary and the Attorney General."**

The example of Jamaica was afterward followed by other colonies in the West Indies. British Honduras also

---

* Alpheus Todd, "Parliamentary Government in the British Colonies," p. 30.

** "Colonial Year Book," 1891, p. 351.

in 1869 surrendered its representative government and became a Crown colony.

Progressive Measures for Political Advancement Should Precede Absolute Self-Government.

The inference to be drawn from these events is that it is unwise to introduce a system of absolute self-government into those colonies which are not entirely prepared to exercise it judiciously. It is incumbent upon trained statesmen to bring about a modification of existing conditions in a gradual and cautious way, by means of progressive measures, which may guide a people, step by step, into new and untrodden avenues of political advancement.

This Spanish statesmen have endeavored to do as regards Cuba and Porto Rico, where "slavery has been abolished almost as early as it was in this country, this great revolution being accomplished after no terrible shedding of human blood, after no long and bitter warfare, but peacefully, quietly, effectively,"* by means of a wise law; and in the same progressive spirit "Cubans have been granted the same rights as other Spaniards; they are represented in the Spanish Cortes; their provincial and municipal administration is surrounded by guarantees; the civil and criminal laws of Spain, administered by tribunals similar to those of the Peninsula, have been established in Cuba; public instruction has been organized upon the same basis as in Spain; the economic legislation for Cuba has been regulated to facilitate the prosperity and wealth of that magnificent portion of America;"** in a word, to quote a phrase before cited, the institutions in Cuba have been rendered, as far as possible, "the very image and transcript" of those of Spain.

Acknowledgment of Cuban Autonomists as to the Enjoyment of Social and Political Rights.

This has been frankly acknowledged by the Autonomist party in Cuba in their manifesto, and one of the eminent leaders of that party, Señor Rafael Montoro, in an inter-

---

* *United States Financial and Mercantile Examiner*, February 6, 1897.

** "Spanish Rule in Cuba: Laws Governing the Island," p. 10.

view with an American journalist in 1895, declared that "to-day all classes in Cuba enjoy the fullest measure of social and political rights."

And yet this sweeping statement was made long before Spain's Prime Minister, Señor Canovas, had drafted the bases of a much more liberal régime for Cuba.

New Reforms Will Establish An Advanced System of Political Autonomy.

By the new reforms Spain will establish in her West Indian possessions a political autonomy adapted to the existing conditions in those islands, which will be greatly in advance of the various systems adopted by other European nations for the government of their respective colonies. In none of the possessions of France, Portugal or Holland is there any form of local administration that can compare with the autonomic measure which the Government of Spain has devised for Cuba and Porto Rico.

The Colonial System of Holland.

In his review of Dutch colonization, the Cuban historian, Señor Labra remarks that Holland until very recently has regarded her colonies as large farms and plantations, establishing in them a system of oppressive exploitation which included the bondage of the Indians, the prohibition from holding lands, military dictatorship, native despotism, the division of race and caste, and mercantile intolerance.* Her colonial system, even in the nineteenth century, has been tyrannical, and tending chiefly to make profit out of the cultivation of lands in Java by means of obligatory cultivation, a system invented by General Van den Bosch with the aid of a trading company. It was only in 1890 that lands, labor and commerce became free to all. Before that time the natives frequently committed suicide or emigrated to escape the horrors of Dutch oppression. "Holland looks upon her colonists as subjects who cannot enjoy the same rights as the mother country, much less govern them-

* R. M. Labra, "La Colouización en la Historia," Vol. II., p. 366.

selves. Following this doctrine her colonies are placed beyond the Constitution of the Realm, they are not represented in Parliament, and they are controlled by the supreme authority of the home Government."*

The Colonial System of Portugal

Portugal, like Spain and France, has adopted the policy of assimilation, giving to her colonial subjects representation in the Parliament at Lisbon and the same civil and political rights as are enjoyed by the Portuguese in the mother country. But Portugal has not given to her colonies any measure of local self-government. Their administration is under direct control of the Parliament at Lisbon, where all the laws for the colonies are framed, notably those referring to civil, political and military organizations, custom houses, banking, coining, &c. The direction of colonial affairs is intrusted to the Minister of Marine, who is also Minister for the Colonies. As an advisory board there is also a Council for the Colonies.

The Colonial System of France.

France, whose colonial domain had acquired such vast proportions under the shrewd policy of Richelieu and Colbert, only to be wasted away as a result of maladministration and the Napoleonic wars, has of late extended her ultramarine possessions, which are now scattered throughout the world, and can be classified under two heads: *Colonies*, over which France exerts absolute sovereignty and which she directly controls, and *Protectorates*, over which France has only a suzerain right, exercising simply a surveillance of their native administration.

French colonies admit of three divisions: (1) Algeria, which rather than a colony is considered as an integral part or prolongation of the territory of France, and is therefore governed as one of the departments; (2) colonies which are represented in Parliament and are assimilated to the mother country, though not in the same degree as Algeria, and (3) colonies in which the administration is in

* La Grande Encyclopædie, Vol. XI., p. 1096.

a very crude and rudimentary state. Among the latter are a number of colonies which have the character of military posts and others which are simply penal colonies.

How Guadeloupe and Martinique Are Governed.

In the second group are included Guadeloupe and Martinique, which enjoy the highest degree of assimilation, and which, being located, like Cuba and Porto Rico, in the archipelago of the Caribbean Sea, merit our special attention as subjects for comparison.

Guadeloupe and the adjoining islands constitute a department represented by thirty-six Councilors General. The Council General elects from among its members a Colonial Committee, composed of not less than four and not more than seven members, and said committee discusses the affairs of the Department with the Governor appointed by the French Government, who is also advised by a Privy Council. The Municipal Councils of the several communes are constituted in the same manner as the Communal Councils in France. The island sends one Senator and two Deputies to Parliament.*

The administration of Martinique is very similar to that of Guadeloupe. The island is represented in Parliament by one Senator and two Deputies, and in the Council General of the island by thirty-six Councilors elected by a very small number of voters, these very rarely taking any interest in the elections.**

"The French Chambers, in accordance with parliamentary usage, are invested with a very extensive right of control over the administration of the colonies, the more so since all the important colonies are therein represented. But Parliament has little occasion to intervene, as the Government, by virtue of a prerogative which has, how-

---

* Réclus, "Geographie Universelle," Vol. XVII., p. 874.

** Ibid.

ever, been contested, frames all colonial legislation by means of decrees."*

Neither in the Dutch, Portuguese or French colonies, therefore, is there to be found a measure of local self administration as broad as the one about to be applied to Cuba and Porto Rico.

The British North America Act of 1867.

The most advanced and liberal system of home rule yet devised for the government of a colony has been implanted in Canada by Great Britain under the provisions of the British North America Act of 1867. But, as has already been stated, this autonomic measure retains for the Crown indirect, if not direct, control over general and provincial legislation in the Dominion, not only by virtue of the veto, but also through the complexion and composition of the legislative power, one chamber being in a measure representative af the Crown.

According to the provisions of said act the Queen appoints the Governor General (Sec. 10), who in turn appoints the Lieutenant Governors of the Provinces. (Sec. 58.) To aid and advise the Governor General there is a privy council, the members of which are chosen, summoned and removed by the Governor General. (Sec. 11.)

The Parliament of the Dominion consists of the Queen, an upper house styled the Senate, and the House of Commons. (Sec. 17.) The Senate consists of seventy-two members, who are appointed for life by the Governor General (Secs. 21, 24, 29), who also appoints and removes the Speaker of the Senate. (Sec. 34.) The House of Commons is summoned from time to time by the Governor General, and can also be dissolved by his authority. (Secs. 38, 50.)

Crown Control Over General Legislation.

All bills passed by both houses are subject to Royal assent. (Sec. 55.) Bills assented to by the Governor Gen-

* La Grande Encyclopædie, Vol. XI., p. 1109.

eral may, within two years, be disallowed by the Queen and consequently annulled. (Sec. 56.)

Provincial Legislation Also Controlled by the Crown.

Quebec is the only province that has two houses in its legislature; they are styled the Legislative Council and the Legislative Assembly (Sec. 71). The legislature of Quebec is a transcript of the Parliament of the Dominion. Councilors are appointed by the Lieutenant Governor for life (Sec. 72); the Speaker of the Council is appointed and may be removed by the same authority (Sec. 77); the Assembly is summoned from time to time, and may also be dissolved by the Lieutenant Governor (Secs. 82, 85), and he assents to or withholds assent from bills passed by the legislature, in Her Majesty's name.*

As regards the Judicature, the Governor General appoints the judges of the Superior, District and County Courts in each province. (Sec. 96.)

It is evident, therefore, that, while allowing full play to home legislation in the Dominion, the Crown still retains supervision and supreme control over provincial legislation, not only by the appointment of the executive officers and, through them, of Privy Councilors, Senators and Legislative Councilors, but also through the assent to or dissent from all bills by executive officers, and lastly through the Crown prerogative of disallowing bills assented to.

Provincial and Municipal Assemblies in Cuba and Porto Rico More Autonomic Than in Canada.

Provincial and municipal legislation in Cuba and Porto Rico, under the new reforms, will be decidedly more autonomic in character than that of the Dominion of Canada. Both provincial and municipal assemblies shall be elective, by popular vote, and "shall have full freedom of action as regards the selection of their presiding officers, as well as in all matters not contrary to law or to the respect due to the rights of private individuals." (Basis I.)

Inasmuch as Cuba is represented by Senators and Dep-

* A. Todd, "Parliamentary Government in the British Colonies," p. 440.

uties in the Spanish Cortes, wherein general legislation is made for the whole nation, no parliament need be established in the islands; but for matters pertaining to home legislation a Council of Administration is created, composed of thirty-five members, of whom twenty-one shall be elected by popular vote among the different provinces, the others being designated in the Decree from among men who are representative by virtue of their office, position or standing. Such are the Rector of the University of Havana, the Presidents of the Chamber of Commerce, the Economic Society of Friends of the Country, the Sugar Planters' Association and the Tobacco Manufacturers' Union, who shall be Councilors *ex-officio;* also the five ex-Senators or ex-Deputies that have been elected to the Cortes the greatest number of times. Finally, the Chapters of the Cathedrals of Havana and Santiago de Cuba shall elect one of the Councilors, the trades or guilds of Havana another, and two more Councilors shall be elected by and from among the two hundred largest taxpayers in the Province of Havana.

Composition of the Council of Administration.

The composition of such a Council, to which all matters relating to taxation, budget of expenses, tariff, banking and education are intrusted, will insure a better and fuller representation of all the various interests in the Island than would be the case if the Governor General were to appoint the Councilors, as in Canada, or if the election of the whole Council were left to the influences and intrigues of electoral wire-pulling.

Advantages of New Regime for the Spanish West Indies.

The policy of assimilation to the mother country, as developed by Spain, France and Portugal, would seem to be best adapted to the government of colonies of the Latin race; yet, in the new régime soon to be implanted in the Spanish West Indies, while their representation and participation in the National Government is maintained, a system of complete self-government is introduced into local affairs by means of the Council of Administration, and the Provincial and Municipal Assemblies, such as will gradually pave the way to a broader form of responsible government. As Señor Canovas points out in the preamble to his Decree, the Reform Law framed by Señor Abarzuza, which the Cortes passed in 1895, "was never to be considered a finality in an evolution initiated by the metropolis with so much forethought and good faith."

More Liberal and Progressive Reforms to Be Expected.

Neither should the broader reforms now planned by Señor Canovas be considered a "finality"; for in the ebb and flow of the political tide in Spain the Liberal party is sure to succeed the Conservative government of Canovas in due course of time, and then the régime now adopted for Cuba and Porto Rico, which will amply satisfy the present needs of the inhabitants of those islands, will make way for reforms still more liberal and progressive, until a complete system of autonomy is obtained.

In implanting the new rule Spain may well say to the Cubans, as Lord Carnarvon said to the Canadians in 1883: "In legislation, in self-government, you are free, and may you ever remain so; but in loyalty to the Crown, in love to the mother country, may you ever be bound in chains of adamant."

Part Second.

Expository Preamble and Royal Decree Sanctioning the Plan for the Extension in Scope of the Abarzuza Reform Law of 1895.—Commentary: Expressions of Opinion by Party Leaders and the Press. —Text of the Abarzuza Law.

By Antonio Cuyás.

EXPOSITORY PREAMBLE.

YOUR MAJESTY: Ever since Your Majesty's confidence was reposed in the present Ministry the war in Cuba has been the object of its constant anxiety, which was later heightened by the rebellion in the Philippine Archipelago. To-day the end of the latter seems to be near; and although no precise date can be predetermined for the ending of the Cuban insurrection, its evident abatement suffices to warrant certain measures in anticipation of and adequate to the probable course of events.

Aims of Cuban Conspirators.

It is important, Your Majesty, that the facts anteceding these events be borne in mind. It is daily becoming more evident that the protracted conspiracy which preceded the war was not entered into with the end in view of obtaining any concessions compatible with Spanish sovereignty, as there exists ample documentary evidence to prove that the promoters of said conspiracy never contemplated anything but the independence of the Island. So manifestly was this their aim that, as is well known, the Reform Law of March 15, 1895, which was supported in the Cortes with such good faith by all political parties, Peninsular and Cuban, far from restraining the revolutionary movement, hastened its outbreak, it being the purpose of the conspirators to prevent the beneficial effects of said law from exerting any direct or indirect influence toward the maintenance of peace. Thus, forcibly, the Spanish nation, which had long before granted to its Antilles all the political rights unanimously accepted by modern civilization, and which, at the very time when its sovereignty began to be combatted, was endeavoring to establish certain reform measures, indisputably liberal and in the direction of self-government, was obliged to take up arms in defence of the integrity of its territory. Some persons were led by their generous spirit to believe at first that by merely putting the reforms into practical operation the plans of the conspirators would be baffled; but the majority of Spaniards soon became convinced that we had to deal with another separatist war, the inefficiency of which would have to be demonstrated before the concessions contained in the Reform Law could give any useful results. To this conviction and to the manifest impossibility—soon afterward created by the war—of introducing a new régime in Cuba, when the established one could barely be enforced, was due the postponement in putting the reforms into effect; a postponement which was not voluntary, therefore, but unavoidable. And since the settlement of the matter was intrusted to the force of arms, not through choice of the mother country, but much against her wishes, it has been necessary for us to wait until arms should determine the precise moment in which to employ other means dictated by reason and justice.

Reasons for Postponement of Reforms.

Of course the Reform Law, which had been approved by the Cortes (Congress), was never to be considered a finality in an evolution initiated by the metropolis with so much forethought and such sincerity. The doubt might have been entertained at one time whether it would have been advantageous even to the residents of the Antilles for them to enter suddenly on an autonomic form of government, in view of the ill effects of precipitate action in such matters.

Evils of Hasty Action in the Matter of Reforms.

Without going further than Cuba, we see that such ill-effects had already been experienced in the matter of the sudden and unlimited freedom of the press, which was so largely instrumental in bringing about the insurrection.

All this notwithstanding, what Spanish or foreign statesman could suppose that where such liberal political rights existed, the mother country would be niggardly in granting administrative reforms to work in harmony with the political laws? No, it could not in good faith be assumed that the Reform Law of March 15, 1895, was a finality. It is evident, on the contrary, that the only limit not to be exceeded in the granting of concessions could and should be no other than that pointed out to Your Majesty's Government by the inexorable duty of preserving the nation's heritage.

The Reform Law of 1895 Not a Finality.

But, as has been seen, to destroy the latter without any regard whatsoever to Spain's historical rights in the premises has been the chief intent of the rebels. They purposely ignored all peaceful means whereby they could, while in the free exercise of political rights, establish an administrative autonomy on solid bases. Instead of that they pandered to the impatient longings of the youth of the land; they excited the most anarchical passions; they denied all value to the advantages already acquired; they fostered the most unconquerable pessimism on the one hand, while on the other they aroused the most chimerical hopes. By such means they succeeded in having the above-mentioned law, which had been so enthusiastically passed by the Cortes, received both in Cuba and Porto Rico with indifference, if not with disdain, and in spreading the insurrectionary conflagration.

Lessons of the War.

Some time has elapsed since those events. The war, with its manifold disasters, has been fruitful in severe lessons to all the well-disposed inhabitants of the Island of Cuba. Nor is it impossible that there should be a reawakening of the fraternal feeling so long dormant, but which among people of the same race can never be entirely extinguished; and certainly the persuasion that, after all, a peaceful and steady progress, though not satisfying every aspiration, is preferable to the triumphs of violence, no matter by whom obtained, is daily gaining ground.

Mistaken Opinion as to Spain's Strength.

Coincident with this there is evidently vanishing the mistaken opinion that Spain would be unable to carry on another war like the former one, an opinion held by those who, basing their judgment on insufficient data, attributed our magnanimity in Morocco to impotency, and who therefore thought that the struggle with the metropolis would be easy and of brief duration. The documents taken on various occasions from the insurgents prove conclusively that at one time even they were led into the same error, they who are our own brothers, and who therefore should never for a moment have doubted the firmness and virility of those of their race in the mother country.

In the meantime it is well known that, although Spain has been compelled, on account of the circumstances above recited, to postpone, and may be still obliged to defer, the carrying into effect of the liberal administrative régime that is essential to Cuba's future prosperity, she has never given up the intention of applying in due time the reforms approved by the Cortes, nor has she failed to appreciate the necessity of broadening their scope in such a manner as to satisfy both the Peninsulars and the Cubans who are shedding their blood on our side in the present struggle, as well as all the inabitants of the Island of Cuba who have the common welfare at heart. And the sincerity with which the new régime will be carried out by the home Government cannot, reasonably, even be questioned. To be convinced of this, we have but to remember the speech pronounced by Your Majesty on the occasion of the opening session of the present Cortes; for no one will doubt the loyalty of Your Majesty's Councilors, whosoever they may be, and, being loyal, it

Spain's Intentions of Applying the Reforms.

would be folly to assume that, whatever their differences of opinion on other matters, they would not all agree in upholding every Royal promise. No; such promises cannot ever be allowed to remain meaningless phrases, nor therefore shall those most solemn ones remain such, whereby Your Majesty offered to confer upon both the Antilles, as soon as the state of war would warrant it, "an administrative and economic personality of a purely local character, but which would assure the unimpeded intervention of all the people of the respective islands in their own affairs, while leaving the rights of sovereignty intact, and unimpaired the conditions necessary for their maintenance."

Spain's Pledges to Be Fulfilled.

From that moment it was not to be questioned that any Spanish Government would shape its course to that end. In regard to the Ministry which is to-day favored with Your Majesty's confidence, it may be said that not only did its several members individually co-operate as efficiently as anyone else toward the approval of the aforementioned Reform Laws, but during the debate on the answer to the last speech from the Crown the present Cabinet, through its President (the Prime Minister), made certain statements which met with the approval of the most liberal of its political opponents, and which the Ministry could not, without jeopardy to its honor, fail to uphold.

Any Spanish Government Would Act Loyally.

One of the statements, Your Majesty, was to the effect that the Government would not wait until the last insurgent had disappeared from Cuba, but that it would deem the moment when the final victory should be assured and the national honor satisfied as the proper time to meet the real necessity felt in Cuba of testing what the English term "self-government," *i. e.*, a liberal decentralization of such a nature as to allow the people of the Island to manage their own interests, and to assume, at the same time, the responsibility of their own acts, relieving the metrop-

The Proper Moment in Which to Establish the Reforms.

olis therefrom. Another of the statements made by the Prime Minister on the same occasion was that, aside from the serious motives hereinbefore mentioned, he was actuated to move, as he proposed moving, in regard to the policy for the West Indies, by a due consideration for the erroneous opinion prevailing in America and in Europe to the effect that we, the Peninsulars, obstinately denied to our brothers in Cuba and Porto Rico that which other nations granted their trans-oceanic provinces, an opinion which entailed upon us considerable injury. Such a notion was and is really most unjust, as is made evident by our colonial traditions and by our own conduct for many years past with regard to the political government of the West Indies. Notwithstanding this, it was not fitting that the Government should scorn this erroneous opinion, but, on the contrary, it deemed it a duty to dispel the causes thereof by practical measures. It never has, in truth, been advantageous for any one country to deviate in its political methods from the general trend of those of other nations, and the history of Spain amply bears out this assertion; and much less can it be advantageous at the present day, when the solidarity of all civilized peoples is such that a mere variance from the forms peculiar to the general system carried out by the predominant nations is usually fruitful of trouble. It is manifest that national dignity will always and in all countries spurn any measure that is not the expression of its own inmost conscience, spontaneously conceived, and much more will it spurn foreign imposition of any sort. But this does not imply that any power should systematically disregard public opinion, which, when legitimately expressed and generally held, is entitled to the same respect from the great human associations as from the individuals constituting them. In a word, Your Majesty, everything urges your Government to the fulfillment of the promises made by Your Majesty before the Cortes,

A Due Regard for Public Opinion.

and which by the Royal sanction, and with the consent of his colleagues, were repeated and extended in scope, also before the Cortes, by the Minister who has now the honor of addressing Your Majesty.

Sr. Canovas del Castillo's Record as a Cuban Reformer.

There is nothing, either, in what he submits for the Royal approval that is not in accord with his own political record. Before anyone else he devoted himself with energy and efficiency to the work of suppressing the slave trade; over thirty years ago he convened an important and illustrious assembly of delegates from the West Indies, intrusted with the task of thoroughly reforming in their respective provinces the then existing régime with regard to the administration of local affairs and to the labor question. After the capitulation of Zanjón he extended to Cuba, with such slight modifications as were at the beginning necessary, the exercise of the same political rights as were enjoyed in the Peninsula; and, lastly, as before mentioned, he contributed, together with all his political followers, without exception, toward the approval by the Cortes of the Reform Law of March, 1895. Such is the record to which the undersigned ventures to call the gracious attention of Your Majesty, not assuredly in a boastful spirit, but in order to strengthen the certitude which the natives of the West Indies should be possessed of that whatever Spain offers she stands ready to fulfill with inviolable good faith. For, if the present Prime Minister speaks now, more particularly in his own name, he hastens to acknowledge and proclaim that all other Councilors invested with Your Majesty's confidence will in the future act in like manner, because Spanish statesmen can differ in regard to this question only in their ability or in the degree of success they may attain, but never in their good faith or in their loyalty in redeeming the pledges made in Your Majesty's name and on behalf of the nation.

With the issuance of this Decree Spain will have completed all that it is incumbent upon her to do in order to hasten the end of Cuba's misfortunes. The rest of the task, *i. e.*, the material and practical application of the reforms, will not depend for its performance exclusively upon the mother country in the future. It will also be necessary that the insurgents, convinced as they must be of the futility of their struggle, and moved to compassion by the desolation and ruin of their native land, lay down their arms soon and allow free play to the inexhaustible generosity of the mother country, ever ready to take them back into her fold. Although such hopes may be cherished as to many of them, perhaps it would be presumptuous to entertain them as to all. For reasons already set forth by Your Majesty's Government, it may be deemed probable that there will not be wanting men who, blind to their own as well as to their country's best interests, will endeavor to prolong, for however brief a period, the deplorable evils which now afflict the Island, imagining, perchance, that Spain will tire of her sacrifices and raise the flag of peace upon any terms, leaving that beautiful land, together with the lives and property of its loyal inhabitants enlisted in our cause, at the mercy of the irreconcilable advocates of separation from the mother country. As to the present Government, it may here be said that no one will ever obtain its co-operation in such a course.

Spain Will Have Done Her Duty.

Spain Will Never Abandon the Island.

But it is time, Your Majesty, to acknowledge that measures of such scope as those herein proposed are not of the kind that in free countries usually come within the attributes of the Executive. Only the manifestly extraordinary nature of the present circumstances could have persuaded Your Majesty's Government to adopt them in the form of a Decree, upon which the Council of State is to be heard, and which is to be duly laid before the Cortes, in order that it may receive from them the utmost legality that it may require. For less obvious reasons other governments have considered themselves compelled to act in like manner, asking afterward for what, borrowing the term from the English, is now called in Spain a "Bill of Indemnity." To have made such a matter the subject of a prolonged and critical discussion while the war is waging would have invited troubles so self-evident that it is needless to particularize them here. Our Constitution itself recognizes in the Crown the right, in the event of a foreign war, both of declaring it and of making and ratifying peace, submitting afterward to the Cortes a documentary report thereon. And although the insurrection in Cuba is not in truth a foreign war, it may well be compared with those of that nature that we have sustained in the past, on account of the vast sacrifices in men and money that it entails upon the nation. There are not lacking, therefore, plausible reasons for proceeding in the same manner that the Constitution provides in the case of a war with an independent state. But the Government is not seeking at all to shirk its responsibility in endeavoring by means of this Decree to facilitate the ultimate accomplishment of peace. As the Cabinet is ready to face its responsibility before the Cortes, the respect in which the latter are held by the former simply induces it to present here excuses the validity of which it is incumbent exclusively on them to decide. In the meantime, as the thirteenth paragraph, Section 45, of the organic law of the Council of State requires that this body be consulted in regard to "any innovation in the laws, ordinances, rules and regulations applicable to our trans-oceanic provinces," the present Ministry shall not fail to meet this essential requirement in a matter of such moment as the one under consideration, even if it be only in order to strengthen its own judgment with that of the supreme consultative body of the Realm.

Why the Cortes Were Not Convened to Pass Upon the Reform Measures.

Not all the problems involved in the government of the West Indies will be solved, however, by means of the Decree herewith submitted. Some of them give us time to seek their solution from the Cortes—a course, moreover, which their exceptional character demands. One of these is in reference to the determination, in a precise and absolute manner, of the expenses necessary to the maintenance of sovereignty, and of all other expenses, aside from those purely local, that shall correspond to Cuba, as fixed charges upon her Budget. This is a matter that must be submitted to the Cortes, as it affects the Peninsular provinces equally with those of the Island.

Other Problems to Be Solved.

Judicial Organization.

Another of the problems referred to above is the one relative to the judicial organization; for, though all judicial functionaries are already included in one civil list with those of the Peninsula, and though some rules are laid down in the present Decree for their appointment to fill vacancies that correspond to the "turn of selection"* for the West Indies, there remain some essential points to be covered by legislative enactment, among others the proportionate share that the West Indies and the other Spanish provinces shall have in the number of aspirants to the national magistracy.

The Electoral Reform.

No reference is made, either, in the present Decree to electoral reform, because certain reasons of a high order bar the introduction by the Government of changes in the existing system for the election of Representatives and Senators, without the concurrence of the Cortes; and

* In almost every branch of the Spanish Government service the officers and functionaries thereof are registered in the respective civil list according to rank and to seniority in each rank; and in filling vacancies in any but the lowest rank, the appointing officer is not only obliged to promote one of those registered in the rank immediately inferior to the one in which the vacancy is to be filled, but he is obliged to follow two alternate "turns," viz., to the first vacancy occurring in any given class he is to promote the employee, officer or functionary heading, as senior, the list of the class next inferior in rank, this being termed the "turn of seniority." To the next vacancy occurring in the same class he may promote, at his discretion, any employee, officer or functionary included in the list of the class next inferior in rank, provided that the person so selected is otherwise legally entitled to promotion, there being certain requirements such as a certain number of years of service in each rank. This is called the "turn of discretionary selection."—(*Translator's Note.*)

because to the above system, which is the primary one, all others relative to Provincial Assemblies and Municipalities have always been subordinate.

When the Reforms Should Be Put in Force.

The Government is not yet in a position to determine how brief or how long the period may be within which the present reforms can be put into effect in Cuba and, consequently, in Porto Rico, although from all the data at hand at the moment of draughting the following Decree the outlook seems very satisfactory and there are many indications that peace is not far off; but, at any rate, the Government feels that it must be prepared to put such reforms into practical operation without delay as soon as may be possible. To this end, therefore, the Council of State shall be immediately consulted, although the Decree of Reforms shall not be enforced until all necessary conditions are complied with. This done, and the intentions of Spain being from this moment known, it is to be hoped that a conciliatory spirit will prevail in the West Indies, thus hastening by easy means that which the country has always longed for; that which the civilized world desires, and that which Your Majesty and the Government, as much or more than anyone else, have striven for in the past and will continue in the future to strive for—a fruitful and lasting peace.

Your Majesty:

I have the honor to be Your Majesty's
Most humble servant,

ANTONIO CANOVAS DEL CASTILLO.

ROYAL DECREE.

Upon the proposition of my Prime Minister, and with the concurrence of the Council of Ministers, in the name of my august son, King Alfonso XIII., and as Queen Regent of the Kingdom, I hereby decree, as follows:

The Measure to Be Submitted to the Council of State.

Sole Section.—The plan for extending the scope of the reforms for the Island of Cuba which were embodied in the law of March 15, 1895, and which plan shall in due time apply as well to the reforms already put in force in Porto Rico, shall be submitted to the full Council of State, for its prompt consideration and report, in accordance with the provisions of Section 45, paragraph 13, of the organic law of that Supreme National Advisory Body.

Given in the Palace on the fourth day of February, in the year one thousand eight hundred and ninety-seven.

MARIA CRISTINA.

The Prime Minister,

ANTONIO CANOVAS DEL CASTILLO.

PLAN FOR THE EXTENSION IN SCOPE
OF THE
REFORM LAW OF MARCH 15, 1895.

Article 1.

The Law of March 15, 1895, relative to Reforms in the system of Government and Civil Administration in the Island of Cuba, shall be extended and given a wider scope in accordance with the following bases, which so far as may be necessary shall be amplified and developed by means of Rules and Regulations.

Powers of the Provincial Assemblies and Boards of Aldermen.

Basis I.—The Boards of Aldermen and the Provincial Assemblies of the Island of Cuba shall enjoy such liberty of action as may be compatible with observance of law and with the rights of private individuals.

They shall be free to appoint and remove all their employees.

The Presidents of the Provincial Assemblies shall be elected by said assemblies from among their own members. In each Provincial Assembly there shall be a Provincial Executive Committee, consisting of Assemblymen elected semi-annually by the Assembly. The Provincial Executive Committee shall elect its chairman.

Mayors: How Elected.

Mayors and Deputy Mayors shall be elected to the respective offices by the Board of Aldermen from among their own members. The Mayors shall without limitation exercise the executive functions of the municipal government, as the executive officers of the Boards of Aldermen.

A Provincial Assembly may stay the execution of resolutions adopted by any of the Boards of Aldermen under its jurisdiction; it may also censure, warn, fine or suspend the members thereof, whenever said members shall exceed the limits of their municipal jurisdiction; in such case the Assembly shall report such action to the Civil Governor for his approval and for its execution.

Should the Civil Governor not approve the action of the Provincial Assembly, either in whole or in part, said Assembly may appeal to the full Supreme Court of the corresponding territory, whose decision shall be final.

The Raising of Revenue.

For the purpose of raising the revenue necessary to meet their expenses and obligations, the Municipal Councils and Provincial Assemblies shall be vested with all the authority compatible with the system of taxation governing the general and local Budgets of the Island; it being understood that the revenues for the provincial Budgets shall be independent of those for the municipal Budgets.

Public Education.

The establishment of public educational institutions in the provinces shall devolve exclusively upon their respective Provincial Assemblies, and of those in the cities and towns upon the Boards of Aldermen.

The Governor General and the Civil Governors shall have the right of intervention in these matters only to the extent necessary to insure compliance with the general laws, and to satisfy themselves that the new charges imposed by the local Budgets are not in excess of the respective provincial and municipal resources.

Financial Statements by the Mayors.

The annual financial statements rendered by the Mayors, which shall include all receipts and expenditures, both ordinary and special, shall be published in their respective localities, and whatever may be their total amount shall be audited, and objected to or approved, as the case may be, by the Municipal Council, after hearing any protests offered against them. From the action of the Municipal Council appeal may be taken to the Provincial Executive Committee, and in cases where the latter shall declare the liability of any official or officials, an appeal may be taken to the full Supreme Court of each respective district, which shall decide, without further recourse, in conformity with the administrative and penal laws that may be applicable thereto.

Basis II.—The Council of Administration shall consist of thirty-five Councilors. Of these, twenty-one shall be elected as follows by the same voters who are entitled to suffrage at the elections for Assemblymen and Aldermen, and according to the provisions of Article III. of the Reform law of March 15, 1895, as follows: Five by the Province of Havana, four each by the Provinces of Santa Clara and Santiago de Cuba, three each by the Provinces of Pinar del Rio and Matanzas, and two by the Province of Puerto Principe. Nine other Councilors shall be the following: The Rector of the University of Havana, the President of the Havana Chamber of Commerce, the President of the Economical Society of the Friends of the Country, the President of the Sugar Planters' Association, the President of the Tobacco Manufacturers' Union, a member of the Chapters of the Cathedrals of Havana and Santiago de Cuba, which Chapters, assembled as electoral colleges, shall elect such member every four years; a representative of all the trades associations of Havana, to be chosen every fourth year by the presidents of such trade associations, and two Councilors representing the principal taxpayers of the Province of Havana, to be elected every four years, one by the hundred citizens paying the highest taxes on real estate and the other by the hundred paying the highest taxes on industries, commerce, arts and professions. The remaining five Councilors shall be the Senators or Representatives to the Cortes who shall have been elected the greatest number of times at general elections, seniority of age determining where other conditions are equal. **Council of Administration: How Constituted.**

The Governor General shall be the *Honorary* President of the Council, and he shall preside, without vote, at any session he may attend. The regular President shall be **President of the Council.**

appointed by the Governor General from among its members.

The Office of Councilor. The office of Councilor shall be without compensation, shall carry personal liability, and, once accepted, cannot be resigned except for cause. The office shall also be incompatible with that of Representative to the Cortes or Senator, and anyone eligible to the two shall elect between them within two months.

Candidates having the qualifications necessary for election as Representatives to the Cortes, and having resided two years on the Island, may be elected Councilors.

In no case shall those debarred from election as Representatives to the Cortes by Section 19 of the Provincial Law, now in force, be elected Councilors.

The Council shall have a Secretary's office, with an adequate force for the transaction of the affairs hereby assigned to it.

Appointment and Removal of the Council's Employees. The power of appointment and removal of all employees of the Secretary's office shall be solely and exclusively vested in the Council.

The Council shall elect every six months a Committee on Reports, whose duty shall be to report upon all matters coming within the jurisdiction of the Council.

Said committee shall consist of five Councilors, each of whom shall be entitled to such compensation as the Council may determine, but which shall not exceed the sum of $2,000 for each term of six months.

Expenses Inherent to Sovereignty. ***Basis III.***—The Cortes shall determine the expenditures, which shall necessarily be chargeable as expenses inherent to sovereignty, and every three years shall fix the total amount of revenue required therefor; this without prejudice to the right of the Cortes to alter this provision.

Levying of Taxes. The Council of Administration shall each year levy such taxes and imposts as may be necessary to provide the total amount of revenue required and to meet the expenditures approved by the Cortes in the national Budget for the Island; this without prejudice to the constitutional right of the Cortes to introduce such changes as it may deem proper in the premises.

The Council of Administration may renounce the powers conferred upon it by the last preceding paragraph; in which case it shall be understood that it also renounces, for the term covered by the Budget, the powers conferred by Sections 1 and 2 of the first paragraph, Basis IV.

Should the Council of Administration surrender said powers, or should it fail on the first day of June of any year to levy the taxes and imposts for the revenue required to meet the expenditures included in the national Budget for the Island, the Governor General shall supply such default, so far as it may exist, and either in part or in whole, through the Chief of the Treasury.

The Council to Prepare Budgets.

The Council of Administration shall also prepare and approve every year the local Budget for the Island of Cuba, in order to make provision for such branches of the public service as are intrusted to it. It shall also include in said Budget the necessary appropriations for the personnel and the supplies for the office of the Secretary of the General Government of Cuba, for the Bureau of Local Administration, for the Department of Finance, for the office of the Auditor, and for the offices of the six Provincial Governors of the Island, which expenses are hereby declared to be obligatory charges upon said Budget.

In regard to the obligatory charges just mentioned, the Governor General shall, should the case arise, become vested with the powers mentioned in the fourth paragraph of the present basis, relative to the national Budget for the Island.

Should any changes or modifications adopted by the Council of Administration affecting services chargeable, as fixed obligations, against the local Budget for the Island, not be approved by the Governor General, they shall be submitted to the Minister for the Colonies for final action, to be taken by resolution of the Cabinet, after first obtaining a report thereon from the Council of State. In default of any action by the Minister within two months, the action of the Council of Administration shall stand.

The Council of Administration shall approve the local Budget for the Island before the first day of June in each year.

Revenues for Local Budgets.

The revenues of the local Budget, besides those already provided, shall consist of such taxes and imposts as the Council of Administration may determine and as shall not conflict with the sources of revenue applied to the national Budget for the Island.

Educational Institutions.

The establishment of new educational institutions preparatory for the various Government services*, the Army and Navy excepted, shall devolve upon the Council of Administration, whenever such institutions shall be of a general character and for the benefit of the entire Island.

The Council of Administration may file with the Governor General claims or protests, should there be occasion for them, against any resolution or action taken by the Chief of the Bureau of Local Administration.

Powers of the Council in the Matter of Customs Tariff.

Basis IV.—The Council of Administration shall have the following powers in the matter of customs tariff:

1. To make, upon the recommendation of the Chief of the Treasury of the Island, the rules and regulations for the administration of the customs revenue.

2. To take such action as it may deem advisable, with the advice of the Chief of the Treasury, or upon his recommendation, in regard to export duties.

3. To fix or change at its discretion, with the advice of the Chief of the Treasury, or upon his recommendation,

---

* See notes on pages 58 and 71.

the fiscal duties to be levied upon imports through the Custom Houses of the Island of Cuba.

4. To report upon and to recommend any changes which experience may suggest in the general or supplementary dispositions of the tariff, or in the schedules, notes or repertory thereof; said report to necessarily precede any action taken thereon.

These powers are granted subject to the following limitations:

Protection to National Products.

1. A reasonable and necessary protection shall be maintained in favor of national products and manufactures, provided they be directly of national origin, as regards their importation into the Island of Cuba; such protection to be accorded by means of differential duties to be levied at the minimum rates, hereafter to be determined, equally upon all products of foreign origin.

2. The fiscal duties to be fixed by the Council of Administration shall not be differential, but must apply equally upon all imports, those of national origin included.

Export Duties.

3. Such export duties as may be established shall not be differential, but shall be applied equally to the same class of products, whatever their destination. Exception may be made, however, in favor of products exported directly for national consumption, in which exclusive case the Council of Administration may grant exemption from or a differential reduction in the duties by it established.

4. The prohibition to export any product, should this at any time be ordered, shall not apply to products exported directly for national consumption.

5. The powers granted by virtue of Sections 1 and 2 of the first paragraph of this present basis shall be exercised by the Council of Administration or, in default thereof, by the Governor General, in accordance with the obligations imposed by the second paragraph, Basis III. The fiscal import duties, and also the export duties, should such be established, shall remain unchanged during the term cov-

ered by the Budget which is based upon the revenues that those duties are estimated to provide.

Form of Customs Tariff.

The import tariff shall be embodied in the following form : The duties shall be set forth in two columns, viz., the first shall contain the fiscal duties to be levied and collected on all importations of whatever origin, national included ; the second shall contain the differential duties to be levied equally upon all products of foreign origin; these last mentioned duties to constitute the necessary protection which is secured to national products and manufactures.

Fiscal Duties.

The fiscal duties comprised in the first or general column may be freely altered by the addition of such extra rates of duties and by such reductions or exemptions as the Council of Administration may determine, in the exercise of the powers hereinbefore granted, subject to the limitations also hereinbefore expressed.

Maximum of Protection.

The Cortes shall determine the maximum of protection to be maintained in favor of national products and manufactures. The maximum thus established shall not be altered without the concurrence of the Cortes, and this concurrence shall also be necessary for any changes in the column of differential duties.

The initial duties to be levied upon all the articles comprised in the various schedules of the tariff and which are to constitute, for the first time, the differential column before mentioned, shall be fixed by the Government.

Differential Duties.

These differential duties, which need not in general be higher than 20 per cent. *ad valorem*, shall not exceed 35 per cent. *ad valorem*, even on such articles as may require this exceptional and maximum rate. A special act of the Cortes shall be required in order to exceed the above limit of 35 per cent. on any article. Such act may raise the limit to 40 per cent. *ad valorem*.

The Government shall order a revision of the official schedules of valuations of merchandise after a full hearing of all interests. Whenever, as a result of the revision of said schedule of valuations, and by reason of the limitations established by the preceding rule, it shall appear that a reduction should be made in the differential duty on any specified article of the Tariff, the finding of said fact shall of itself operate to effect such reduction. The official schedules of valuation of merchandise, once revised, shall remain unchanged for the term of ten years, unless otherwise provided by the Cortes.

Revision of Schedules of Valuation.

It being impossible to carry immediately into effect all the provisions that this basis establishes for the future, and it being deemed inadvisable to further delay the revision of the Tariff now in operation in Cuba, the Minister for the Colonies shall, by virtue of legal authority now vested in him, and in accordance with the law of June 28, 1895, publish and put into effect a provisional Tariff, the general lines and the schedules of which shall be adjusted to the requirements of this present basis; and the fiscal duties which may be thus fixed and which may appear in their respective column, and also whatever may relate to export duties or regulations, shall be provisionally put into force.

Provisional Tariff.

Commercial treaties or conventions which shall affect the customs tariff of the Island of Cuba must be of a special character. The benefits of the clause of the "most favored nation," or any equivalent thereof, shall not be granted therein. The Council of Administration shall be consulted as to the advisability of granting any special concessions which the Government may have in view, in negotiating any treaty, before the latter shall be completed for submission to the Cortes.

Commercial Treaties.

Basis V.—The Governor General shall have the power to appoint and remove all the employees of the office of the Secretary of the General Government of the Island, of the Bureau of Civil and Economic Administration and

Power of Appointment of Employees.

of the Provincial Governments, as provided in Basis VII.

Basis VI.—The office of the Secretary of the General Government shall be under the direction of a Superior Chief of Administration.

Chiefs of Bureaus to Nominate Appointees.

The Chief of the Treasury of the Island of Cuba, the Comptroller and the Chief of the Bureau of Local Administration shall propose to the Governor General the appointment of all the employees of their respective offices, according to the provisions of Basis VII., and they may likewise propose their removal.

Postal and Telegraph Service.

The Bureau of Posts and Telegraphs, under the direction of a Chief of Administration, shall have under its charge the services relative to postal and telegraphic communications, both land and maritime, for which the Council of Administration may make provision; and it shall be its duty to examine and render annually the accounts of said services and to execute all the resolutions of the Council concerning the Bureau.

Employees to Be Natives or Residents of Cuba.

Basis VII.—All the employees of the Civil and Economic Administration of the Island of Cuba, with the exception of the Secretary of the General Government, the Chief of the Treasury, the Comptroller, the Chiefs of the Bureaus of Local Administration and of Posts and Telegraphs, and the Civil Governors of the six Provinces, shall be appointed, as vacancies occur, by the Governor General of the Island of Cuba, in conformity with existing laws or with such as may be hereafter enacted, from among the natives of said Island or from among others residing or having resided there during two consecutive years.

The Governor General shall submit to the Council of Administration, for its cognizance, evidence of the legal qualifications of all appointees.

In the appointment of all functionaries belonging to the

civil service professions* and to the postal and telegraph service, the legal dispositions and rules and regulations relating thereto shall be complied with.

Civil Service Provisions.

The employees of the office of the Secretary of the General Government and of the offices of the Provincial Governors shall be appointed and removed by the Governor General at his discretion. The employees of the Bureau of Local Administration, of the Treasury and of the Administration of Customs (except in case a corps of experts be organized) and of the office of the Comptroller, shall be appointed by the Governor General upon the nomination of the respective chiefs of the above mentioned branches of the service. They may be removed by the Governor General upon the proposition of said chiefs, or directly by the former whenever he shall deem it necessary.

Supervisors of Public Education.

The Governor General may appoint Supervisors of Public Education; two each for the Provinces of Havana, Santa Clara and Santiago de Cuba, and one each for the Provinces of Pinar del Rio, Matanzas and Puerto Principe.

Deputies to Represent Civil Governors in Towns.

The Governor General may also appoint, upon the nomination of the Provincial Governors, Deputies representing the latter authorities in the municipal districts. Said Deputies shall have gubernatorial authority in their respective localities and shall have control of the police

* Various branches of the Government service in Spain constitute what are termed state or civil service professions. Admission thereto can only be obtained through a special course of studies for each, and after a rigid competitive examination for such vacancies in the lowest rank as from time to time are to be filled. Once admitted, members of said professions cannot be removed from office, except after trial for cause, though they may be assigned to different posts pertaining to their respective ranks; and their advancement is regulated by a system which, while securing to all equal justice in promotion by seniority, still offers to all an incentive to zeal and efficiency. See note on foot of page 58. At a certain age, and after a given number of years' service, members of civil service professions may retire with a pension, proportionate to their rank on retirement.—*Translator's Note.*

force. In no case shall they interfere with the Mayors or Boards of Aldermen in the exercise of their powers.

The Governor General, whenever he shall deem it advisable, and acting upon the recommendation of the Provincial Governors, may in the same manner deputize the Mayor of any city or town.

Administration of Justice.

Basis VIII.—Any vacancies which may hereafter occur in any of the offices under the Administration of Justice* and the appointment to which may, according to turn, be discretionary,** shall be filled by the Minister for the Colonies, either from natives of the Island of Cuba or from those who reside or may have resided there. Applications for appointment, accompanied by the records of the respective applicants, shall be filed with the Presidents of the Supreme Courts of the various districts, and shall be forwarded to the Department through the Governor General.

Municipal Judges.

The Municipal Judge of each judicial district shall be appointed by the Governor General, who shall select for that office one of three persons to be nominated by the Aldermen of the respective municipalities and by the voters entitled to vote for the electors of Senators, regard being had to the provisions of the law relative to the appointment of electors.

In municipalities where two or more Judges are to be appointed separate ballots shall becast for each set of nominees in the manner above provided.

The Municipal Judges who may be elected must possess the qualifications prescribed by the existing laws in the Island of Cuba.

Council to Respect Pending Contracts.

Basis IX.—The Council of Administration shall respect pending contracts throughout the various branches of the

---

* This comprises Judges and Prosecuting Attorneys.—*T. N.*

** See note foot of page 71.

Government service and of the Treasury of the Island, and upon their expiration may renew them or not at its discretion.

The Council of Administration is hereby empowered to apply to the Island of Cuba the Law regulating the operations of the Treasury which is now in force in the Peninsula, and to enter into an agreement for that purpose with the Spanish Bank of the Island of Cuba.

Council Empowered to Contract for Collection of Taxes.

The Council is further empowered to intrust the above mentioned Bank with the collection of revenues, or to contract with it with reference thereto, subject always to the approval of the Minister for the Colonies.

Basis X.—A special Decree, which shall be reported to the Cortes, shall contain such dispositions as may be deemed necessary for the preservation of the public peace and for the suppression of any separatist movement which by any means whatever may be again set on foot.

Preservation of the Public Peace.

Article 2.

The Government shall embody in a single instrument the foregoing provisions and the provisions of the reform law of March 15, 1895, so as to harmonize the two; and shall in due time report the same to the Cortes.

Previous and Present Reform Measures to Be Adjusted.

These united provisions shall be supplemented by rules and regulations to be subsequently formulated, which, however, shall in no manner change the intent or meaning thereof, and whose sole purpose shall be to adjust the said provisions to other legislation now in force, as provided in the before mentioned law of March 15, 1895.

Upon the issuing of an order putting into effect in Cuba the provisions of the law of March 15, 1895, and the provisions of this Royal Decree, said provisions shall, so far

These Dispositions to Have the Force of Law.

as may be possible, have all the force of law, without prejudice to the rules and regulations subsequently to be made.

Article 3.

Reforms Applied to Porto Rico.

The provisions of the present Decree, as an extension in scope of the law of March 15, 1895, shall be applied to the Island of Porto Rico wherever compatible with the different conditions prevailing in said Island and with the institutions already established there.

The rules and regulations already issued for Porto Rico shall be amended so far as may be necessary to bring them into accord with those which shall be issued for the Island of Cuba.

Article 4.

When the Reforms Shall Be Put Into Effect.

The date upon which the provisions of the reform law of March 15, 1895, shall be put into effect in Cuba, and upon which the provisions of this supplementary Decree shall be applied to both Cuba and Porto Rico, shall be determined by the Government as soon as the condition of the war in Cuba shall permit.

The Prime Minister,

ANTONIO CANOVAS DEL CASTILLO.

MADRID, February 4, 1897.

The Reform Law of March 15, 1895, to Be Referred to In Connection with the Present Measure.

The dispositions of the foregoing Royal Decree being directed to the modification and extension in scope of the Reform Law of March 15, 1895, a proper understanding of the former requires that the latter be referred to, and for this purpose the text in English of that law is hereunto appended. See page 87.

COMMENTARY.

Points to Be Borne in Mind in Reading the Foregoing Decree.

IN perusing the official text of the "Expository Preamble" and "Royal Decree" embodying the reform measures recently adopted by Spain for the government of the Island of Cuba, which is herein rendered in as faithful an English version as the difference in construction of the two languages would permit of, the reader will undoubtedly have a better comprehension of those measures and a more adequate appreciation of their scope if he will bear in mind: First—The political complexion of the party whose leader, as Premier of the Kingdom, has prepared and obtained the sanction of the Crown for such a radical measure of Spanish colonial policy. Second—The purpose which has actuated Her Majesty's Government in adopting such a course, and its intentions as to the development and application of the plan of reforms. Third—The view taken in regard to this plan by the leaders of other Spanish political parties. Fourth—The spirit in which its announcement has been received in Cuba by prominent natives and influential Peninsular-born residents. Fifth—The trend of public opinion in foreign countries on the reforms.

As an aid, therefore, to those not thoroughly acquainted with the subject, the writer here presents, supplemented by a few remarks of his own, various statements and expressions of opinion covering the points above enumerated, which he has culled, extracted and rendered into English, where necessary, from such matter as he has at hand.

As to the first point, it is well to remember that while the Conservative party, under the leadership of the present

Prime Minister, Señor Canovas del Castillo, has always, true to its name and creed, opposed radical legislation and the adoption of political measures for which it did not consider the time ripe nor the people of Spain prepared, it has almost invariably, when called into power, respected or "conserved" all successive political rights enacted into the Laws of the Realm through the initiative of the Liberal party. And in many instances, as in the present Cuban question, the Conservatives have forestalled the more advanced party in the granting of reforms, going even beyond the limits predetermined by the latter's declarations of principles as to certain issues.

Conservative Party Forestalls the Liberals in Granting Reforms.

Thus, not only did the Conservative party, then in the opposition, heartily support and solidly vote in favor of the Abarzuza Cuban Reform bill, draughted and submitted to the Cortes by the Liberal Cabinet of Premier Sagasta in 1895, but now, while under the tremendous responsibilities inherent to power in such critical circumstances as Spain is going through, Señor Canovas boldly steps far beyond the boundaries pointed out by the promises of other Spanish statesmen or even by the demands of the several Cuban legal political parties, the Autonomist party alone excepted.

Intentions of the Government.

In regard to the second point, Señor Canovas del Castillo made the following statement on the day in which the Royal Decree was published in the *Gaceta de Madrid* (official organ of record). These utterances of the eminent Spanish statesman confirm and throw additional light on that noble and remarkable official writing : the "Expository Preamble" to the Royal Decree.

To a press representative Señor Canovas said :

I have devoted much study and thought to the preparation of the plan of reforms, and being inspired by the utmost sincerity I have endeavored to imbue the measure with the broadest spirit.

It has been my aim to make of the reforms a national undertaking; I have worked on them, therefore, on behalf of my country and for my country.

Sr. Canovas del Castillo's Statement.

My idea, my determination, is to put them into effect according to the most liberal interpretation and with absolute sincerity.

With entire good faith I am resolutely going toward the establishment of autonomy in Cuba. On this line no radicalism can check me. What I have been most careful of is not to leave any loophole for independence. And in this I have fulfilled my duty.

* * * * * *

Application of the Plan of Reforms.

It is not necessary to await the complete pacification of the Island of Cuba in order to put the reforms into practical operation.

As soon the rebellion is reduced to the Oriental Department all the pacified provinces shall immediately enter upon the enjoyment of the advantages to be derived from the new measures. Without further delay the Boards of Aldermen and the Provincial Assemblies shall be elected in those provinces, and they shall have entire liberty of action without any Government intervention. And thus the entire plan of reforms shall be rapidly developed, with a view of having it in practical operation in as short a period as possible.

Sr. Dupuy de Lome's Statement.

In connection with this same point, *i. e.*, the intentions of the Spanish Government as to the development and application of its plan of reforms, it will be proper to transcribe here the statements made by the Spanish Minister in Washington, Señor Dupuy de Lôme, to a representative of The United Associated Presses on the 7th of last February.

A close study of the course of the Cuban question could not but convey to the least observing mind the conviction that this most efficient and able diplomat enjoys to more than an ordinary degree the confidence of his Government. It is but fair to assume, therefore, especially if it be remembered how discreet and cautious have been all Señor Dupuy de Lôme's utterances, that in the following statement the Spanish representative reflects the purpose of his Government; or, in other words, that he gives, *unofficially*, expression to certain knowledge, *officially acquired*, bearing on the question under review.

His statement, in substance, as published is as follows:

Electoral Reforms.

The electoral reforms were not referred to at length in the decree of the Ministry, for the reasons stated in the preamble of Señor Canovas, that they will require the action of the Cortes. I am informed, however, that the Government will not oppose the extension of the basis of the suffrage, but they desire to do it in such a way as to prevent undue influence being acquired by the illiterate portion of the population.

The present law requires the payment of taxes amounting in the aggregate to $5, except where the privilege of voting is extended to the graduates of the universities and other members of the learned professions. Any educational qualification which may be suggested by the Cubans, and which seems reasonable and proper, will undoubtedly be adopted by the Cortes. The subject must be regulated by that body.

It is the purpose of the Government to show the greatest generosity toward the insurgents who lay down their arms. The reforms cannot well be put into full effect until the sovereignty of Spain is acknowledged. The Government will not relax its military activity in any degree if the insurgents show a disposition to continue the contest and fail to appreciate the great concessions made by the home Government.

Spain's Generous Spirit in Dealing with Cuba.

Spain has gone to the utmost limit in her generosity to the Cuban people, and has established a system by which the Island will hereafter be governed in Cuba by residents of the Island, instead of being governed from Madrid. The right to hold office is given to Spaniards who have lived two years in Cuba, because they have become in a large degree identified with the interests of the Island.

In this respect the proposed policy is not unlike that which has been pursued by the United States, where members of both political parties have delighted to honor citizens born outside of the country. Conspicuous examples are found in the cases of Mr. Wilson, of Iowa, who is to be a member of the Cabinet of your next President, and who was, I believe, born in Scotland, and of Carl Schurz, who was born in Germany, but was Secretary of the Interior under the administration of President Hayes.

The tariff features of the new Decree are very comprehensive in their scope, and mean a great deal for the United States as well as for Cuba. The duties levied will be equal against all countries except Spain; and American manufacturers and exporters, in view of their familiarity with Cuban trade and their nearness to the Island, are likely to appreciate the importance of these concessions.

The Tariff Features.

The situation will be much more favorable to American trade than under the reciprocity treaty of 1890. There were in that treaty two schedules for American goods, one of 25 per cent. and another of 50 per cent., but Spain had the right to provide for the entry of her products free of duty, thus giving her a marked advantage over the United States. The Spanish West Indies are the best consumers of United States products that you have on this continent. It will be necessary for the home Government to consult the Cubans before a reciprocity treaty is concluded. The new reforms distinctly provide that such treaties may be suggested by the new Council of Administration.

More Favorable to the United States than the Reciprocity Treaty.

The Council of Administration shall not only contain twenty-one members elected by the qualified voters of Cuba, but will contain Cubans among the other members, if they possess the qualifications to attain the position which entitles them to seats. The members of the Council of Administration, who shall sit by virtue of their office as Presidents of the Chamber of Commerce, the Planters' Association and other bodies, may just as well be Cubans as persons born in Spain, if they show the qualities which naturally advance them to those places. The places are entirely open to native Cubans as well as Spaniards.

The Liberal party, upon returning to power, could or would never attempt to take a step backward on such a vital national issue, either by reactionary legislation or by a narrow interpretation of the measures enacted by the Conservatives.

The Liberal Party Indorses the Plan of Reforms.

That is not only self-evident, but it is assured beyond peradventure by the fact that the leaders of the Liberal party have approved of the new plan of reforms. In effect, Señor Maura, who in colonial matters can speak with best authority on behalf of said party, he being the author of the Reform bill of 1893, has said:

The Royal Decree issued by the Prime Minister unfolds with vigorous frankness a system which differs much more radically from that now established in the West Indies than did the Law of 1895* or the Bill of 1893.** It adopts principles and lays down bases which should satisfy all aspirations, that are not insatiable, of the liberal political parties in Cuba. I spurn as absurd any insinuation to the effect that the scope of the reforms may be impaired by the rules and regulations and other means for their application, because no statesman should be insulted by imputing such bad faith to him, nor would any fail to perceive the dangers of so acting.

The Republicans Also.

The present reform measures also meet the favor of the Spanish Republicans, as is evidenced by the following words from their leader, the great orator, Don Emilio Castelar:

> I, as a writer, can only applaud the tendencies of the reform decrees. I approve them with all my heart, and support them with all my power. I oppose any design of reducing them, whatever be its origin.
>
> With the projects of Maura, Abarzuza and Canovas, all defended by me, we have dealt justice to Cuba, establishing her self-government and developing her commercial relations.
>
> From them good, nothing but good, can come. Therefore I am satisfied, and thus you have my opinion.

The Cuban Autonomists Approve of the Reform Measures.

As to how the reforms will be accepted by the political parties in Cuba, by influential organizations of the Island and by Cuban public opinion in general, the following excerpts from statements thereon may give a fair idea. Those from the leaders of the Autonomist party, who are also Members of the Cortes, are of the utmost importance, because the principles and ideals of this party undoubtedly represent the aspirations of the majority of native residents of the Island, and because it is more than likely

* In force in Porto Rico, but not yet applied to Cuba on account of the insurrection.

** Of which Señor Maura, then Minister for the Colonies, was author, but which did not become law on account of his leaving the portfolio.

that to its banners shall rally the better class of those who have participated in the present insurrection, as soon as the latter is finally put down.

Here are the extracts above referred to:

From Señor Rafael Montoro, a native of Cuba, one of the leaders of the Autonomist party and Member of the Cortes for the Island:

Statement of Sr. Montoro.

A New Era Is Dawning.

It is difficult to make quite clear to the Anglo-Saxon mind what will be the political relations in Cuba to the mother country in the new era which is dawning. It is impossible to reason by analogy and contrast with the British colonies, because, to cite merely one cause of essential difference, Spain has a written Constitution which is the palladium and supreme guarantee of our liberties, and Great Britain is ruled by a more flexible and an unwritten Constitution.

Our Constitution establishes a certain identity of civil and political rights between all subjects of the Crown, and it provides that we Cubans must have our representatives in the Cortes, as do all other provinces of the kingdom.

Suffrage in Cuba is Sufficiently Ample.

Our suffrage for the election of Deputies to the Cortes is even now, in my opinion, sufficiently ample, but it will be even more extensive under the new régime, so that the voice of Cuba may be heard on all questions of finance and of foreign affairs which interest and affect alike all portions of the kingdom.

In connection and in harmony with the Local Assembly of Cuba there is no room for doubting that the national or imperial Cortes will grant to us the fullest powers of self-administration and self-government that are possible under our Constitution and compatible with the unity of the Kingdom.

The Reasonable Demands of the Cubans Fully Satisfied.

I think that the Spanish Government will have fully satisfied every reasonable and practical demand of the Cuban people. I expect that then the respectable but misguided elements of the insurrection will withdraw from the field, and that there will remain under arms only lawless adventurers and irreconcilable enemies of law and order.

Adjustment of the War Debt Not an Insurmountable Obstacle.

The question of the adjustment of the indebtedness ensuing out of the war is, I admit, a difficult one, perhaps the most difficult one which the situation presents, but it is not an insuperable obstacle to peace, as some especially ill-informed publicists in foreign countries represent it to be.

I believe the subject can be reasonably and equitably settled by an arrangement between the Spanish and Cuban treasuries.

Also from Señor Montoro, on another occasion, conjointly with Señor José A. del Cueto, likewise a prominent member of the Autonomist party:

In our opinion the reform measure is of the utmost importance, since the institutions based thereon are remarkably liberal, and the changes introduced in the present system are very radical. If understood and loyally appreciated they reveal the noble fulfillment of the promises contained in the Crown Speech and explained in the memorable summing up of the debate in the Cortes on the 15th of July last by Señor Canovas.

The New Measure Contains All Essential Elements of Self-Government.

We believe that the above measure contains all the essential elements of self-government, and that the amendments and extensions in scope that it may require in order to reach all the development possible within the national Constitution may well be left to the action of time, of public opinion and of local initiative, when, peace being restored, it will become possible for them to manifest themselves authoritatively. The Expository Preamble of the Royal Decree opens reasonable horizons to every loyal aspiration in that direction.

The effects of the reform measure upon the public spirit cannot but be very favorable at the present moment, and they shall be more so according as the intentions of the Government become known.

Sr. Labra's Statement.

From Señor Labra, a distinguished Cuban jurist, Autonomist Member of the Cortes for the Island:

Señor Canovas' plan of reforms implies a laudable change in the course of our colonial policy. It is necessary that we work on that basis. We may now expect from the Liberal Peninsular party a new determination and a more decided spirit in its attitude and in its course, since the step in advance taken by the Conservative party is really an exceptional one.

Autonomy the Best Guarantor of the Nation's Integrity.

As for me personally, I may say that I have never been pessimistic in politics, and that I have to-day additional reasons for reaffirming what I have always held, that colonial autonomy is the best guarantor of the honor, the strength and the integrity of the nation.

Sr. Fernandez de Castro's Statement.

From Señor Rafael Fernandez de Castro, a Cuban Autonomist, ex-Member of the Cortes for the Island :

The reforms represent a great progressive stride in Spanish colonial policy. They are more liberal than those embodied in the Reform Law of March 15, 1895, and of course more of a fundamental nature than those prepared in his bill by Mr. Maura in 1893. They are equivalent to a grand and decisive entry into a régime that the wise nature of things has been demanding here for some time; that of Autonomy.

A Great Progressive Stride.

From Señor Arturo Amblard Member of the Cortes for the Island of Cuba:

Sr. Amblard's Statement.

I believe that the reforms will completely satisfy the long felt wishes of the people of Cuba, and that although they contain details of secondary importance that in practice will be corrected, they may be the means of bringing together many men hitherto of clashing opinions, and of gaining supporters to the national cause.

From Señor Rabell, leader of the Cuban Reformist party, in a cable dispatch to Premier Canovas:

Sr. Rabell's Congratulations.

The executive committee of Reformist party, upon learning of reform measures, has resolved to compliment Your Excellency for the broad spirit that they reveal. By such consistent action Your Excellency will satisfy the legitimate aspirations of the people of this Island, who confidently expect the development of the plan of reforms, with the sincere co-operation of all the loyal elements of Cuba, in order to bring about peace, which everyone desires.

The general applause with which the reform measures have been received is the best evidence of their merit.

From Marquis of Apezteguia, a native of Cuba and leader of the Union Constitucional party (this, being the "Tory" or Conservative party of the Island, has always opposed reform measures for Cuba in the direction of self-government):

Statement of the Cuban Conservative Leader.

The Union Constitucional party cannot oppose the work of the Government. I have come to the Peninsula for the purpose of avoiding friction and in the interest of harmony. As to the effects of the reforms in Cuba, I believe that they will have none directly upon the insurgents in arms. But the new measures will appeal to the reason of the pacific native elements and to foreigners in general, and this moral

The Cuban Conservative Party Will Not Oppose the Reforms.

force on our side will undoubtedly weaken the direct or indirect support that the insurrection has received in some countries.

Voice of the Havana Chamber of Commerce.

From Señor Rosendo Fernandez, President pro tem. of the Havana Chamber of Commerce:

I am positive that this Chamber of Commerce will nobly aid the Government in every measure tending to the attainment of peace and to the fostering of the moral and material interests of the Island on the indisputable basis of Spain's sovereignty.

The Produce Exchange in Favor of the Reforms.

From Señor Marcelino Gonzales, President of the Havana Produce Exchange:

The reforms having been studied out and prepared by so eminent a statesman as Señor Canovas del Castillo, and embodying, as the press reports show, such liberal measures of self-government, they cannot but be beneficial to commerce in general, which shall have more within reach the means of overcoming the obstacles it may encounter in the development of its foreign trade.

Favorable Opinion of the Importers' League.

From Señor Laureano Rodriguez, President of the Cuban Importers' League:

It is my opinion that the reforms, after a revision of the electoral census (enrolment), when put into operation in a spirit of good faith, will satisfy the aspirations of the inhabitants of this Island.

The following comments are culled from Cuban and foreign newspapers:

From *El País*, organ of the Autonomist party:

The Cuban Press.

The reforms should be received with satisfaction and applause, and they should meet with our sincere co-operation, for they go much further in the direction of self-government than the plans of either Señor Abarzuza or Señor Maura.

From the *Diario de la Marina*, organ of the Reformist party:

Thanks to the reforms we can now confidently say that the misfortunes of the Island of Cuba are soon to end.

From *La Lucha*, Republican organ:

The time has come for every honest man who has the welfare of Cuba at heart to exert all his influence and all his endeavors toward convincing those who are at present in arms that there exists no longer the reasons or the pretexts with which they pretended to justify their rebellion.

From *La Union Constitucional*, organ of the party of that name (Conservative):

The Union Constitucional party will not set any obstacles in the way of the solutions which the home Government has prepared to the difficulties that beset out common country.

From *El Diario del Ejercito*, organ of the army:

Señor Canovas has once more shown the deep interest he takes in Cuban affairs by granting the Island such reforms as the spirit of the times and the public requirements demanded.

From *Le Gaulois*, of Paris:

The Foreign Press.

As a whole the reforms planned by the Madrid Government are of a nature calculated to satisfy the aspirations of Cubans. If the latter should not consider themselves satisfied they would forfeit the sympathy of European nations, who understand perfectly that the Spanish Government in granting to Cuba such liberal laws has gone in one bound to the limit which its dignity and its duty would allow.

From *L'Eclair*, of Paris:

We must admit that in these circumstances Señor Canovas has not revealed himself a Conservative after the fashion of Guizot, who remained unmoved even while he foresaw progress. Señor Canovas resembles rather the great British Conservative Robert Peel, who in 1846 did not hesitate to split his party in order to grant political liberties to the British people.

From *Le Temps*, of Paris:

If Señor Canovas del Castillo considers it necessary to grant to Cuba ample concessions it is, in the first place, because the urgency of establishing the reforms has appeared perfectly clear to him, and, in the second place, because he is perfectly satisfied that he can put them into effect without prejudice to Spain's honor or Spain's interests.

REFORM LAW OF MARCH 15, 1895.

LAW FOR THE REORGANIZATION OF THE GOVERNMENT AND CIVIL ADMINISTRATION OF THE ISLAND OF CUBA.

Alfonso XIII., by the Grace of God and the Constitution, King of Spain, and, in his name and during his minority, the Queen Regent of the Kingdom: To all whom these presents shall come, know ye that the Cortes have decreed and we have sanctioned the following:

ARTICLE I. The system of government and the civil administration of the Island of Cuba shall be readjusted on the following bases:

BASIS I.

Provincial Assemblies and Municipalities.

The laws of municipalities and of provinces now in force in the Island are hereby amended to the extent necessary for the following ends:

The Council of Administration shall, upon the report of the Provincial Assemblies, decide all questions relating to the formation of municipalities, and to the determination of their boundaries.

The law of provinces is hereby amended as to the matters placed by these bases within the powers of the Council of Administration.

The Provincial Assembly shall decide all questions pertaining to the organization of Boards of Aldermen, to their election, to the qualification of the members and other similar questions.

Each Board of Aldermen shall elect one of its members as Mayor. The Governor General may remove a Mayor and appoint a new Mayor, but the new Mayor must be a member of the Board. In addition to their functions as executive officers of the Boards of Aldermen, the Mayors shall be the representatives and delegates of the Governor General.

Whenever the Governor General shall stay the resolutions of a municipal corporation* the matter shall be laid before the criminal courts, if the stay be due to misdemeanor com-

* See note page 97.

mitted by the corporation in connection with the resolutions, or laid before the Provincial Governor, upon the report of the Provincial Assembly, if the resolutions were stayed because they exceeded the powers of the Board, or because they infringed the law.

The Provincial Governors may stay the resolutions of the municipal corporation, and censure, warn, fine or suspend the members of the corporations when they exceed the limits of their powers.

Previous to removing Mayors or Aldermen, in the cases provided by law, the Governor General must give the Council of Administration a hearing upon the removal.

Every member of a municipal corporation who shall have presented or voted in favor of a resolution injurious to the rights of a citizen shall be under a liability, enforcible before the court having jurisdiction, to indemnify or make restitution to the injured party, the liability ceasing according to the rules of the Statute of Limitations.

Municipal Taxation.

Each Board of Aldermen shall, in matters defined as within the exclusive municipal powers, have full freedom of action, agreeably with the observance of the law, and with the respect due to the rights of citizens. In order that the Boards of Aldermen and the guilds* may fix the amount of the taxes to cover the expenses of the municipality and may determine their nature and their distribution, in accordance with the preference of each municipality, the Boards of Aldermen and the guilds shall have all the powers necessary thereto, that is compatible with the system of taxation of the State.

The Provincial Assemblies may review the resolutions of municipal corporations relating to the preparation or alteration of their estimates of revenues and expenditures, and, while respecting their discretionary powers, shall see that no appropriation which exceeds the assets be allowed, and that arrears of previous years and payments ordered by courts having jurisdiction have the preference. The Governor General and the Provincial Governors shall in these matters have only the intervention necessary to insure the observance of the law and to prevent municipal taxation from impairing the sources of revenue of the State.

The annual accounts of each Mayor, inclusive of revenues

---

* For purposes of *taxation* the various trades are formed into guilds. Taxes on trades are apportioned among the guilds, whose officers fix the tax to be paid by each member according to the valuation of his business.

and expenditures, ordinary and extraordinary, shall be published in the municipality and audited and corrected by the Provincial Assembly, after hearing protests, and approved by the Provincial Governor if they do not exceed 100,000 pesetas, and by the Council of Administration if they exceed that sum. The Provincial Assemblies and the Council of Administration shall determine if any officials have incurred liabilities, except in the cases that come within the jurisdiction of the ordinary courts.

Appeals to the Council of Administration may be taken from the decisions of the Provincial Assemblies.

BASIS II.

The Council of Administration shall be organized as follows: **The Council.**

The Governor General, or the acting Governor General, shall be President of the Council.

The Supreme Government shall appoint by Royal Decree fifteen of the Councilors.

The Council shall have a staff of secretaries, with the personnel necessary for the transaction of its affairs.

The office of Councilor shall be honorary and gratuitous.

Councilors Appointed by the Crown.

For appointment as Councilor the appointee must have resided in the Island during the four years previous to appointment, and must have one of the following qualifications:

To be or to have been President of a Chamber of Commerce, of the Economic Society of Friends of the Country, or of the Sugar Planters' Association.

To be or to have been Rector of the University, or Dean of the Corporation of Lawyers of a provincial capital for two years.

To have been for the four years previous to appointment one of the fifty principal taxpayers of the Island, paying taxes on real estate, on manufactures, on trade, or on licenses to practice a profession.

To have been a Senator of the Kingdom or a Representative to the Cortes in two or more legislatures.

To have been two or more times President of a Provincial Assembly of the Island; to have served for two or more terms of two years as member of the Provincial Executive Committee;* or to have been a Provincial Assemblyman eight years.

To have been for two or more terms of two years Mayor of a provincial capital.

To have been, until the proclamation of this act, member of the Administrative Council for two or more years.

The Council may, whenever it shall deem it expedient, summon to its deliberations, through the Governor General, any chief of department, but the latter shall not vote with the Council.

Councilors Elected by the People.

To form the Council fifteen additional Councilors shall be elected by voters having the qualifications requisite to vote for Provincial Assemblymen.

The term of office shall be four years. The elections to fill vacated seats shall take place every two years, the Provinces of Havana, Pinar del Rio and Puerto Principe voting at one election, and the Provinces of Matanzas, Santa Clara and Santiago de Cuba voting at another.

The Province of Havana shall elect four Councilors; the Province of Santiago de Cuba shall elect three; and each of the other provinces shall elect two.

All the Councilors shall be elected at the same time: upon the establishment of this act, and after a total removal of the Council. Two years after the establishment of this act, or after a total removal of the Council, the Councilors from the first group of provinces above named shall vacate their seats, and their successors shall be elected.**

In ordinary cases the election shall take place at the same time as the elections for Provincial Assemblymen, the votes for Councilor and for Assemblyman being cast together.

The Council shall be the judge of the elections, returns and qualifications of the Councilors-elect and of the qualifications of the Councilors appointed by the Crown, and shall decide all questions concerning its own organization under the law.

BASIS III.

The Council of Administration shall resolve whatever it may deem proper for the management in the whole Island;

---

* Each of the six provinces of Cuba—like every other Spanish province—has a Provincial Assembly. The Assembly meets twice a year in sessions of about two weeks, and appoints from its members a Provincial Executive Committee (*comisión provincial*) to act during the intervals between the sessions.

** At the next election the Councilors elected for the second group of provinces would vacate their seats.

of public works, posts and telegraphs, railways and navigation, agriculture, manufactures, trade, immigration and colonization, public instruction, charities and the health department, without prejudice to the supervision and to the powers inherent to the sovereignty of the nation, which are reserved by law to the Supreme Government.

Powers of the Council.

Each year it shall prepare and approve the estimates with sufficient appropriations for all those departments. It shall exercise the functions that the laws of provinces and of municipalities and other special laws shall attribute to it. It shall correct, and in the proper cases approve, the accounts of its revenues and expenditures, which accounts shall be rendered every year by the general management of the local administration,* and shall determine the liabilities therein incurred by officials.

The local revenues** shall consist of :

Revenues.

1. The proceeds of Crown lands and rents, and of the institutions whose financial management pertains to the Council.

2. The surcharges which, within the limits fixed by law, the council may add to the taxes imposed by the State.

It shall be the duty of the Governor General, as superior chief of the authorities of the Island, to carry out the resolutions of the Council.

For that purpose the general management of the local administration, as delegate of the Governor General, shall attend to the departments included in the local estimates and shall keep the books thereof and shall be responsible for the non-fulfillment of the laws and of the legitimate resolutions of the Council of Administration.

Whenever the Governor General may deem any resolution of the Council contrary to the law or to the general interests of the nation, he shall stay its execution, and shall of his own motion take such measures as the public needs—which would otherwise be neglected—may require, immediately submitting the matter to the Minister of the Colonies.

If any resolution of the Council unduly injures the rights of a citizen the Councilors who shall have contributed with their votes to the passage of the resolution shall be liable, before

---

* An office in charge of a superior official that under the Governor General act as the executive of the Council of Administration.

** Revenues of which the Council of Administration may dispose.

the courts having jurisdiction, to indemnify or make restitution to the injured party.

Suspension of Members of Council.

The Governor General, after hearing the Council of Authorities, may suspend the Council of Administration, or, without hearing the Council of Authorities, may suspend individual members of the Council of Administration as long as a number of Councilors sufficient to form a quorum remains:

1. When the Council or any one of its members transgresses the limits of its legitimate powers, and impairs the authority of the Governor General or the judicial authority, or threatens to disturb the public peace.

2. For a misdemeanor.

In the first case the Governor General shall immediately inform the Supreme Government of the suspension, so that the latter may either set it aside or, through a resolution adopted by the Council of Ministers within two months, decree the removal. If at the expiration of the two months the suspension has not been acted upon, it shall, as a matter of right, be deemed set aside.

In the second case, the matter shall come before the court having jurisdiction, which shall be the full Supreme Court of Havana, and its decision therein shall be final. In other cases the accused may appeal.

Advisory Powers of Council.

The Council shall have a hearing:

1. Upon the general estimates of expenditures and revenues of the Island, which estimates, prepared by the Finance Department of the Island, shall be submitted yearly, together with the changes suggested by the Council, during the month of March, or earlier, to the Minister of the Colonies.

Although the Supreme Government may have varied the estimates before submitting them to the Cortes for appropriations to meet the expenses of the departments and the general obligations of the state, it shall always submit with them, for purposes of information, the changes suggested by the council.

2. Upon the general accounts, which the Finance Department of the Island must without fail submit annually within the six months following the end of the fiscal year, and which shall include the revenues collected and the expenditures liquidated.

3. Upon the matters pertaining to the patronage* of the Indies.

4. Upon the decisions of Provincial Governors which shall come on appeal before the Governor General.

5. Upon the removals or suspensions of Mayors and Aldermen.

6. Upon other matters of a general nature.

The Governor General may demand of the Council the reports he may desire.

The Council shall meet in ordinary sessions at stated intervals, and in extraordinary session whenever the Governor General may summon it.

BASIS IV.

Powers and Duties of the Governor General.

The Governor General shall be the representative of the National Government in the Island of Cuba. He shall as vice-royal patron exercise the powers inherent to the patronage of the Indies. He shall be the Commander-in-Chief of the Army and Navy stationed on the Island. He shall be the delegate of the Ministers of the Colonies, of State, of War and of the Navy. All the other authorities of the Island shall be his subordinates. He shall be appointed and removed by the President of the Council of Ministers, with the assent of the Council.

In addition to the other functions which pertain to him by law or by special delegation of the Government it shall be his duty:

To proclaim, execute and cause to be executed, on the Island, the laws, decrees, treaties, international conventions and other mandates that emanate from the legislature.

To proclaim, execute and cause to be executed the decrees, Royal orders, and other mandates that emanate from

---

* In England when lords of manors first built and endowed churches on their lands they had the right of nominating clergymen (provided they were canonically qualified) to officiate in them. This right is the "patronage" (*jus patronatus*). The Bulls of Alexander VI. in 1493 and of Julius II. in 1508 granted the Crown of Spain the patronage of the Indies (New World). It includes not only the right of presentation to the churches and monasteries built and endowed by the Crown, but other rights so extensive that the author speaks of the Kings of Spain as the "born delegates of the Holy See and apostolic vicar-generals in the Indies."—*Translator's Note.*

the executive, and which the Ministers, whose delegate he is, may communicate to him.

To suspend the proclamation and execution of resolutions of His Majesty's Government, when in his judgment such resolutions might prove injurious to the general interests of the nation or to the special interests of Island, informing the Minister concerned of the suspension, and of the reason therefor, in the speediest manner possible.

To superintend and inspect all the departments of the public service.

To communicate directly upon foreign affairs with the representatives, diplomatic agents and consuls of Spain in the Americas.

To suspend, after consultation with the Council of Authorities, the execution of a sentence of death, whenever the gravity of the circumstances may require it, and the urgency of the case be such that there is no opportunity to apply to His Majesty for pardon.

To suspend, after consultation with the same Council, and on his own responsibility, whenever extraordinary circumstances prevent previous communication with the Supreme Government, the constitutional rights expressed in Articles IV., V., VI. and IX., and Sections 1, 2 and 3 of Article XIII. of the Constitution of the State, and to apply the Riot Act.

It shall also be the duty of the Governor General as head of the civil administration:

To keep each department of the administration within the limits of its powers.

To devise the general rules necessary for the execution of the laws and regulations, submitting them to the Minister of the Colonies.

To conform strictly to the regulations and orders devised by the Supreme Government for the due execution of the laws.

To determine the penal institutions in which sentences are to be served, to order the incarceration therein of convicts, and to designate the jail liberties when the courts order confinement therein.

To suspend any public official whose appointment pertains to the Supreme Government, giving the Government immediate notice of the suspension, with the reasons therefor, and to fill *pro tempore* the vacancy in accordance with the regulations now in force.

To act as intermediary between the Ministers, whose delegate he is, and all the authorities of the Island.

The Council of Authorities shall consist of the following members: The Bishop of Havana or the Reverend the Archbishop of Santiago de Cuba, if the latter be present; the Commander of the Naval Station, the Military Governor, the presiding justice of the Supreme Court of Havana, the Attorney-General, the head of the Department of Finances, and the director of local administration. Council of Authorities.

The resolutions of this Council shall be drawn up in duplicate and one of the copies shall be sent to the Minister of the Colonies. They are not binding upon the Governor General. All his acts must be upon his own responsibility.

The Governor General shall not surrender his office nor absent himself from the Island without the express order of the Supreme Government.

In case of vacancy, absence or inability the Military Governor shall be his substitute, and in default of the latter the Commander of the Naval Station, until the Supreme Government appoints a *pro tempore* Governor General.

The criminal part of the Supreme Court at Madrid shall have the sole jurisdiction over the Governor General for infractions of the Penal Code. Charges of maladministration against the Governor General shall be brought before the Council of Ministers.

The Governor General shall not amend nor revoke his own decisions when they: have been confirmed by the Supreme Government; or have vested rights; or have served as the basis of a judgment of a court, or of the adjudication of a mixed juridical administrative tribunal; or when he bases his decision upon the limitations of his powers.

BASIS V.

The civil and financial administration of the Island, under the supervision of the Governor General, shall be organized in accordance with the following rules: Civil and Financial Administration.

The Governor General with his staff of secretaries, which shall be under the direction of a chief of department, shall attend directly to matters of government, the patronage of the Indies, conflicts of jurisdiction, public peace, foreign affairs, jails, penitentiaries, statistics, personnel of the departments, communication between all the authorities of the Island and the Supreme Government, and all the other matters that are unassigned.

The Finance Department, which shall be under the charge of a superior chief of department, shall attend to the whole management of the finances; it shall keep the books, and audit and submit the accounts of the estimates of the State on the Island.

The provincial administrative sections shall be under the direct control of the Finance Department, without prejudice to the supervision that the Governor General may delegate in fixed cases to the Provincial Governor.

The general management of local administration, under the charge of a superior chief of administration, shall attend to the departments that shall be supported with the appropriations made by the Council of Administration; it shall keep the books, and audit and submit the annual accounts of the estimates of the Council and of the municipalities, and shall enforce the resolutions of the Council of Administration.

The personnel of the offices and the methods for the transaction of affairs shall be adapted to the object of obtaining the greatest simplicity in the transaction of affairs and in fixing official responsibility.

The rules of law shall determine the cases in which a right is vested through the decision of a superior official in a matter that, in accordance with this basis, falls within his jurisdiction, so that an action before the mixed juridical-administrative tribunal may lie.

Nevertheless the injured party may at any time bring a complaint before the Governor General in matters which concern the Finance Department and the general management of local administration, and also before the Minister of the Colonies in any matter that concerns the administration or the government of the Island; but the complaint shall not interrupt the administrative process, nor the legal procedure, nor the course of the action before the mixed juridical-administrative tribunal.

The Governor General and the Minister of the Colonies, when using their powers of supervision, either on their own initiative or owing to a complaint, shall refrain from interrupting the ordinary course of affairs, as long as there be no necessity of taking measures to remedy or prevent irreparable damage, before the final decision of the competent authority.

———

ARTICLE II.*

ARTICLE III. The system of election and the division of the provinces into districts for the provincial elections shall be

---

*Article II. of this act refers exclusively to Porto Rico. Article III. refers both to Cuba and to Porto Rico.

modified by the Government. in order to enable minorities in both Cuba and Porto Rico to have representation in the municipalities and in the Provincial Assemblies, and in Cuba in the Council of Administration of Cuba, and in order to apply to the election of Aldermen, Provincial Assemblymen and Councilors of Administration—in so far as the qualifications of voters and the annual formation and rectification of the registration lists are concerned—the provisions of the Royal Decree of December 27, 1892, upon the reform of the electoral law for the election of representatives to the Cortes, Articles XIV., XV. and XVI. of the said Royal Decree shall be extended to all classes of elections.

For all electoral purposes the taxes imposed by the Council of Administration in Cuba, and by the Provincial Assembly in Porto Rico, by virtue of the new powers granted to them by this act, shall be computed as if imposed by the State.

ADDITIONAL ARTICLE.

The Government shall render to the Cortes an account of the use it makes of the powers hereby granted to it.

TRANSITIONAL PROVISIONS.

1. The Councilors of Administration elected in the Island of Cuba upon the proclamation of this act shall stay in office until the first election for Provincial Assemblymen that happens after two years have passed since the first election of the Council.

2. The rectification, according to the methods that shall be established under Article III. of this act, of the registration lists for the election of Aldermen and of Provincial Assemblymen in both Cuba and Porto Rico, and of Councilors of Administration in Cuba, shall commence from the time of the proclamation of this act.

The Minister for the Colonies shall ordain, by Royal Decree, the necessary measures, and shall fix the time for the various operations of the rectification, so that it may be finished before any election take place to establish the Council of Administration in Cuba or to fill the seats of members of municipal corporations whose terms have expired.

The election for the latter purpose shall under no circumstances be postponed, except in the case of the Boards of Aldermen,* which, in this present year, and if the Supreme

* Municipal corporations in Cuba, as in the Peninsula, have a Board of Aldermen (*ayuntamiento*) and a Municipal Council (*junta municipal*).

Government deem it necessary, may be postponed until the first fortnight of next June.

In subsequent years the rectification shall take place in the manner provided by the Royal Decree of December 27, 1892, referred to in Article III. of this act.

Therefore:

We order all the courts, justices, chiefs, governors and other authorities, civil, military and ecclesiastical, of whatsoever class or dignity, to keep, and cause to be kept, fulfill and execute this act in all its parts.

Given in the Palace, March 15, 1895.

I, THE QUEEN REGENT.

The Minister for the Colonies.

BUENAVENTURA ABARZUZA.

Part Third.

Political and Social Condition of the Island of Cuba.—Statistics of its Wealth and Commercial Movement.—Its Progress Under Spanish Rule Compared with That of Independent Spanish-American Countries.

By L. V. Abad de las Casas.

NOTE—The following paper was written by Señor Abad de las Casas, a Cuban Autonomist, in New York, in 1896, before Señor Canovas framed the new plan of reforms which appears in Part II. of this volume, and it is now published as written, the author's views having been confirmed by subsequent events and strengthened by his experience and observations during his recent travels through Spanish-American countries.—THE PUBLISHERS.

I.

IN view of the determined efforts of certain of the newspapers of this country to convert the insurrection of a part of the Cuban people into an American question;

Of the partisan campaign which is being carried on with that object by certain penny journals, which seem to have made it their aim to deprave public taste and discredit journalism by their sensational articles on all subjects, without previously investigating them, and by their illustrations like circus posters, which are veritable crimes against art;

Of the campaign that, personally, in meetings or by means of pamphlets written in English, the agents of the insurrection are unceasingly carrying on for the purpose of misleading and influencing public opinion by the circulation of Spanish and Cuban news, which, if not always false, is at least exaggerated or partial in a sense favorable to their aims;

And even of the efforts of certain politicians of this country who, through party interest or personal ambition, have made a trade of villifying Spain in their speeches and writings, wilfully or ignorantly misrepresenting the facts, with the same purpose of misleading public opinion, thereby proving how little they care about involving the country in international conflicts in which the people, who do not live by politics, must always lose;

In view, then, of this treacherous and malicious propaganda, I have resolved to write these papers, which I trust the people of the United States will read with enough attention to enable them to perceive that they are inspired only by the desire of making known the truth, in order that the question may be judged with a full knowledge of the facts.

A Cuban by birth and an advocate of self-government for the Spanish provinces of the Antilles and the Philippine Islands since the time when I first took part in Cuban politics, I can assure my readers that they will find in these pages neither a panegyric of the Spanish Government, whose system of administration I have always combatted, and which is the cause of many of the evils which the Cubans suffer, nor a eulogy of my fellow countrymen, who are themselves in no small degree to blame for these evils.

In the majority of the articles published in English which treat of Cuba the impression is sought to be conveyed more or less plainly, according to the amount of conscience the writer still has left, that the question of the independence of Cuba from Spain is similar to that of Greece from Turkey, at the beginning of the present century—an error which has the result of arousing in the public mind, easily influenced and more or less romantic, a feeling of sympathy toward the insurgents, thus converted into heroes of romance, and of prejudice against Spain.

It is true that, on the other hand, other writers, with less feeling perhaps, but with more conscience and more talent, have presented the question under another and more impartial aspect; but the articles of these writers, not sensational enough for the readers of the cheap newspapers, have appeared in reviews, or in newspapers of a serious character, whose readers have less need of exact information, as their higher mental culture enables them more easily to distinguish the true from the false.

Of course the first mentioned writers represent the

Spaniards as barbarians, incapable of comprehending a word of political science or modern law, and the Spanish soldiers as vandals.

In a pamphlet written, it is to be said, in very bad English, I have read the following:

"During her rule of 400 years Spain has not taken a single step tending to the development of the country or to the well-being of the people."

This statement would be merely ridiculous if the author (who was born in Cuba) did not show in making it that his bad faith is even greater than his ignorance of Cuban affairs, which is, however, great enough.

In fact, to suppose that the University of Havana, one of the oldest universities in America; the Economic Society of Friends of the Country, established under the protection of Governor Las Casas in 1793, and the position which Cuba holds, as the foremost among all the Ibero-American countries in culture and material prosperity, are not due to Spain, or to the children of Spaniards born in Cuba, who are also Spaniards so long as Cuba does not change her nationality, is the height of fanaticism, for none but a fanatic could make such absurd allegations.

But if the insurgent propagandists make charges so false and ridiculous against Spanish civilization in America, it shall be my pleasure to remind my readers that a distinguished North American writer, Mr. Arthur R. Marshall, in one of his works on anthology draws attention to the solicitude of Spain for her American possessions, to which she carried her culture, her political science, her literature, her arts and sciences, in contrast to the species of indifference with which England always regarded her North American colonies; so that while the golden age of English literature scarcely found an echo in New England, the Spaniards founded universities and colleges in Mexico, Peru, Ecuador, New Granada, Venezuela and Havana as early as the sixteenth century, which produced men of letters whose fame became universal.*

The Cubans are descendants of either Spaniards or Indians or negroes, or they are of mixed blood; in this case also they are the children of foreigners, who in general marry the daughters of Spaniards.

Those who deny their ancestors and ridicule them abroad, in order to justify the ideal of freedom, which is in itself lofty and noble, and requires no sophisms to defend it, may be shrewd business men, but they show plainly that they are not good patriots, for he who dishonors his ancestors cannot honor his country.

If the insurgent propagandists should say that they desire absolute independence from Spain because they represent a majority of the population of the country, which considers that it possesses the necessary conditions to constitute itself an independent state, then the work of the Cubans who have other political ideas would reduce itself to ascertaining which of the political parties is in the majority, and then giving their support either to their rebellious countrymen or to the Spanish Government.

But in view of the campaign which the propagandists are making those Cubans who, like myself, disown false statements and misrepresentations of facts which are in this case both illogical and base, should also disown the calumnies propagated against the Spaniards, and state facts as they really are.

To enter, then, upon our subject: Remaking history, the insurgent propagandists represent our forefathers, the conquerors of America, as utterly ferocious in their instincts and cruel in their methods of government.

The chivalrous and disinterested, loyal and generous character of the Spanish people, even in mediæval times, when the passions were intensified by the religious ideals

---

*Arthur Richmond Marshall; *The Nation*, New York, January 3 and 10, 1896.

of the age, is proverbial; and although even the casual reader may find in the history of Spain, as in that of France and England, barbarous and sanguinary deeds, yet in no nation—and this nothwithstanding the fact that there existed in Spain for three centuries a religious tribunal which condemned many unhappy persons to the stake or the torture—were so many capital sentences executed, nor was the number of the victims of religious fanaticism so great as in the northern nations of Europe.

In Spain there has never been any prison with a history similar to that of the Tower of London or the Bastille.

Naturally the Spanish adventurers who exposed their lives in open boats to go to unknown countries were not savants who went to America to botanize, in the same way as the men who landed in New England did not go there to botanize.

To prevent the evils which emigration might bring with it, laws were enacted for the protection of the Indians, and that Spain did not employ a policy of extermination toward them is evident from the fact that the region of America which up to seventy years ago was governed by Spanish laws has at the present time a population of 18,000,000 of Indians of unmixed blood.*

The American people, knowing as they do the characteristics of the American aborigines, and knowing also that in all the vast territory of the Union, according to the census of 1890, there remained only 249,000 Indians, while there were still in 1870 350,000, cannot fail to perceive that if Spanish laws had tended to the extermination of the Indians, the customs inherited by the Spanish-

* According to the official statistics of the following republics the approximate number of Indians in each of them is as follows: Mexico, 3,700,000; Guatemala, 850,000; Honduras, 250,000; Salvador, 300,000; Nicaragua, 200,000; Costa Rica, 50,000; Colombia, 700,000; Venezuela, 1,000,000; Ecuador, 600,000; Brazil, 8,000,000; the Argentine Republic, 1,000,000; Uruguay, 130,000; Paraguay, 70,000; Bolivia, 1,750,000; Peru, 1,400,000, and Chili, 50,000.

Americans would not of themselves have sufficed to cause the survival of this enormous contingent of the race which scientists are agreed in saying tends to disappear from the face of the earth.

The names of Commander Ovando and of one or two other Governors are often cited, and history has condemned them severely for their cruelty to the aborigines; but the repeated mention in histories and works of fiction of the same rulers is the best proof that they were the exception to the rule; as in the modern history of Cuba only two governors (Tacon and Lersundi, who by their arbitrary acts greatly prejudiced the cause of Spain) are thus mentioned.

It was precisely the philanthropic sentiments of an eminent monk, Bartolomé de las Casas, toward the American aborigines that caused him to advocate the introduction of negroes into America, as a means of exempting the Indians from labor, which they performed only under coercion, owing to their general refractoriness to adapt themselves to European civilization. In the United States, also, there has been given the opportunity to verify this fact. The social evils which slavery brought to Cuba were caused necessarily by the character of the Indians themselves and of their civilization.

No serious historian has stated that there were 800,000 Indians in Cuba in the fifteenth century, as another pamphleteer asserts, who employs his pen in favor of the insurgent cause, and who represents that backward race as a model of all the virtues, as the sole descendants of Abel, and the inhabitants of an Eden without the serpent.

The Indians have disappeared from the Antilles because they were few in number, for it is well known that they lived in perpetual conflict with the ferocious Caribbee Indians, who decimated their numbers; many of them went to Yucatan and thence to the Mexican deserts, beyond the pale of the civilization which they rejected; the rest became gradually amalgamated with the invading white and black races, and the descendants of these mixed races are frequently to be met with in Cuba, Santo Domingo and Porto Rico.

In a report presented to the King of Spain in 1522, the number of Indians then in the Island was estimated at 5,000. As the number of negro slaves that had been introduced into the Island was much larger than this (in 1774 there were 40,000 African slaves in Cuba), the disappearance of the aboriginal race is not to be wondered at.

Señor Montoro, an eminent Cuban, a member of the Autonomist party in Havana, and a Deputy to the Spanish Cortes in various legislatures, defended his Autonomist opinions in a lecture on Cuba, given in the Athenæum in Madrid, basing them precisely on the ancient Spanish laws, called the Laws of the Indies, and declaring that at that period the principle of self-government for America was accepted in the mother country.

"By virtue of this condition," says Señor Montoro, "the new kingdoms (of America) were organized like those of the Peninsula, *but with their own institutions*, although they were analogous to those of the mother country, and, when the case admitted of it, identical, but separate or distinct from them. I will mention, as an instance, the system of government of the municipalities which, in the first period of colonization, had more attributes and powers than those which the Peninsula enjoyed in the Middle Ages, the period in which municipalities with self-governing powers were organized. The 'Juntas de Procuradores' were very similar to what the Insular Chamber to which we aspire to-day would be."

The laws enacted in 1530 and 1540, in the reign of Charles I., ordained the assembling of Congresses—real Congresses—in Mexico and Peru, conferring on the principal cities privileges analogous to those which Burgos, in Castile, enjoyed.

As another proof that the Spanish policy toward the colonies has not always been retrogressive, I will quote a passage from a discourse pronounced in the Spanish Cortes by Señor Labra, one of the leaders of the Autonomist party.

" See, if this be not so, how in the Island of Cuba, the only country to which I need now refer, public spirit is awakened in the eighteenth century, at the same time that a humane, equitable and provident measure in commercial legislation is initiated (the decree of Charles III., in 1765, establishing free trade with the Colonies); the never-to-be-forgotten General Las Casas, a man of exceptionally advanced ideas of reform, is sent there; and the Economic Society of Friends of the Country is founded, with powers and attributes so ample that it organizes and directs public works and education, fosters agriculture, industry and trade, and thus becomes a sort of Department of Public Works, directing and administering, under the authority of the Governor General, those important branches on which the prosperity and civilization of new countries depend."

It is true that these liberal institutions were afterward lost, as they were lost by the mother country itself, in consequence of the various political crises through which it passed, and which brought with them the decadence of the kingdom.

Cuba being a part of the Spanish monarchy and peopled to-day by the Spanish race, the evil times in the nation's history should not be the only ones to be recalled. Let also the good times be remembered, or none at all.

The invasion of Napoleon produced the first revolutions of America, which, because of the failure of the Spanish rulers to understand them, became converted into wars of independence. The very independence of the United States, accomplished thirty years before, had of necessity a part in this change of ideals; but it must not be forgotten, as it is not forgotten by the American republics, which are to-day the friends of Spain, that it was not motives of dissatisfaction with the sovereignty of Spain that produced this premature dismemberment of territories that were not yet prepared to become independent states; but, on the contrary, a sentiment of loyalty to the Bourbon dynasty, as events demonstrated later.

II.

After this terrible struggle just referred to of the Spanish people with the greatest captain of modern times, a struggle which was for Napoleon the beginning of the Odyssey that was to terminate in St. Helena, Spain awoke to the revolution that had been effected in the social and political order of the world, and took the part in it which belonged to her.

A Congress was elected and Cuba was not forgotten by the Government. Cuba had its representatives in the first Spanish Cortes, and in this fact a principle of justice and an eminently liberal spirit are to be recognized, which were shown by no other nation.

The restrictive policy of 1836 deprived the Antilles of this right and of the enjoyment of many other liberties, producing in the Island the first feeling of dissatisfaction with the mother country.

Then followed a period of difficulty in the development of the social and political life of Spain, characterized, in regard to her colonial policy, by an indecision in every act that might change the manner of life of the colony, and in her political conduct by a disregard of former codes and laws, a policy which produced among the Cubans, as a natural consequence, the discontent which engendered in some of them, influenced by the recent examples of independence on the continent, selfish desires and ambitious hopes.

For this reason various attempts were made at revolution at that period, but these were always isolated and were suppressed in time, rather because the country in general enjoyed a prosperity which was not enjoyed by the continental republics, and did not sympathize with the revolutionary movements, than because of the ability of her Governors.

And in fact the population of the Island, which was 170,000 in 1774, had increased in 1860—less than a century —to 1,200,000.

The trade of the Island, from $15,000,000 in imports and $13,000,000 in exports in 1826, had increased, the former to $43,500,000, and the latter to $57,500,000; that is to say, a commercial movement of $101,000,000, or $85 per capita annually.

In 1862 the total value of the plantations and stock of the Island amounted to $380,554,527; thus the public expenses were covered with the greatest facility, the principal sources of revenue being the 2 per cent. tax on the rents or net produce of rural real estate; 4 per cent. on urban real estate, various small taxes and the customs, subject to a tariff which was highly defective, but which nevertheless produced to the public treasury from 16 to 35 per cent. ad valorem on imports.

At this time not only was there no public debt, but there was a surplus fund of two or three millions in the treasury, and for some few years Cuba contributed an equal amount to the national revenue.

This latter fact, which the insurgent propagandists have loudly proclaimed, and often with exaggeration, need cause no surprise when we consider that Cuba, from 1493 to 1823, was a source of expense to the national treasury;

that is to say, that its budget of expenditures was greater than that of its revenues, so that Spain had to supply the deficiency.

And finally, for public instruction there were eighteen high schools and, between public and private, 468 lower schools, with an attendance of 20,000 pupils.

At this time the Revolution of September, 1868, took place in Spain, and with it a change in the institutions of the country, and a very radical one in the principles of the Government.

At the same time another revolution broke out in Cuba, with the cry of independence, which was as inopportune as it was fatal to the destinies of Cuba.

This revolution, which a year before, when there were as yet no hopes of reform, might have been justifiable, for it would have been the outbreak of a people who could endure no longer the unjustifiable and seemingly interminable state of tutelage in which it was kept, occurring at this period of national evolution proves how lacking both in political wisdom and in patriotism were its leaders.

Plunged at once into a civil war which lasted for ten years, all hope of the reforms which the Island would have had immediately, if the war had not broken out, was cut off, and that war was at the same time highly prejudicial to the development of a broad and liberal policy in Porto Rico.

In spite of this, however, when in 1869 the Cortes of that year was elected on the basis of universal suffrage, this right was granted to the people of Porto Rico, and, making use of it, they sent their Deputies to the Spanish Cortes.

At the same time the Constitution of the State was extended to that Island.

Provincial Assemblies were organized with powers to make and vote the Budgets of the Island for the departments of public instruction, public works (public improvements in general) and other departments, besides having the inspection of the municipalities, which, according to the municipal law, extending also to Porto Rico, were organized on the basis of a popular vote and presided over by Mayors elected by the people ; and slavery was abolished.

That is to say that Porto Rico entered, at the same time with the Peninsular provinces, on the enjoyment of the new political and civil life which was being developed in Spain.

Thus, there is no reason to doubt that but for the war of insurrection the Spanish Government would have extended to Cuba the same liberties and guarantees which it conferred on Porto Rico.

On the other hand, it is also certain that had it not been for the Cuban insurrection Porto Rico would not, five years later, have been deprived of those rights until the Cuban war should terminate.

I think I have demonstrated that the leaders of that movement either sought in it the gratification of personal ambition, rather than the happiness of their country, or else showed a lack of political wisdom which, had the insurrection triumphed, would have been even more fatal to the destinies of Cuba than the loss of the thousands of lives and the millions of dollars which the war entailed.

The war lasted ten years and terminated with a capitulation in which amnesty for past offenses was proclaimed; and it was declared that there were neither victors nor vanquished; the Government promised a liberal rule, and the country, as Señor Cabrera, of Havana, well says in one of his interesting works, wearied and impoverished, sought consolation in hopes of the future.

In regard to the treaty, as it was signed, and to the demands made by the rebels, many inexact statements have been published.

One of these statements was made by an American General, who desired to give it the weight or authority of his name, because he had fulfilled a diplomatic mission from the Government of the United States to that of Spain twenty or twenty-five years ago.

The General referred to stated in a newspaper article that peace was made on the basis of autonomy for Cuba, than which nothing could be more untrue, as the political idea of this system of Government for Cuba had not been conceived until after the pacification of the Island.

Señor Enrique Collazo, one of the insurgent leaders, in his work "From Yara to Zanjón," referring to the willingness of the insurgents to accept peace, speaks as follows:

"Consequently a meeting of the leaders and officers was convoked, and the question being discussed it was resolved to put it to a vote, for which purpose the forces and the people in the encampment were assembled, and Brigadier Rafael Rodriguez explained clearly to them the situation and the object regarding which they were consulted. 'A vote is to be taken to decide on the acceptance of peace or the continuance of war,' he said. 'Let those who desire the latter leave the ranks and form in front; let those who desire peace remain in their places.' *Not one left his place.* The votes of the officers were taken in writing by the same Brigadier Rodriguez, and the Brigadier Benitez and two other chiefs were the only ones who voted for war."

The propositions presented to General Martinez Campos by the committee appointed by the rebels to treat for peace were the following:

First—Assimilation of the Spanish Provinces, with the exception of conscription.

Second—General amnesty for political offenses committed since 1868 up to the present time (1878) for those who are under direct indictment or serving sentences within or without the Island. A general pardon to deserters from the Spanish army, without distinction of nationality; this clause to be extended to all who have taken part, directly or indirectly, in the revolutionary movement.

Third—Freedom for the slaves and Asiatic coolies now in the insurgent ranks.

Fourth—No individual who, by virtue of this capitulation, shall submit to and remain under the authority of the Spanish Government shall be compelled to render military service of any kind until peace be established throughout the Island.

Fifth—Anyone who may desire to leave the Island shall be allowed to do so and be furnished with the means therefor, without passing through any town, if he shall so desire.

Sixth—As a guarantee to our party we request that General Martinez Campos shall hold the civil and political command of the Island for at least one year after the conclusion of peace and the establishment of the reforms consequent on this agreement.

Seventh—The capitulation of each force shall take place in an uninhabited spot, where the arms and other munitions of war shall have been previously deposited.

Eighth—In order to further the acceptance of these conditions by the insurgents of the other departments, the Commander-in-chief of the Spanish Army shall furnish them free transportation by land or sea, over all the lines within his control, to the Central Department.

Ninth—The pact made with the Central Committee shall be deemed to have been made with all the departments of the Island which shall accept these conditions.

The text of the treaty, as it was accepted by the insurgents and signed by the commissioners, is as follows:

CAPITULATION OF ZANJÓN.

The people and the armed forces of the Central Department and the armed groups from other departments having met in convention, as the only fit means of terminating in one sense or another the pending negotiations, and having considered the propositions submitted by the Commander-in-chief of the Spanish Army, determined on their part to propose amendments to said propositions by presenting the following articles of capitulation:

Article I.—The political, organic and administrative laws enjoyed by Porto Rico shall be established in Cuba.

Art. II.—Free pardon for all political offenses committed from 1868 to date (1878) and freedom for those who are under indictment or are serving sentences within or without the Island. Amnesty to all deserters from the Spanish army, regardless of nationality; this clause being extended to include all those who have taken part, directly or indirectly, in the revolutionary movement.

Art. III.—Freedom for the Asiatic coolies and for the slaves who may be in the insurgent ranks.

Art. IV.—No individual, who by virtue of this capitulation shall submit to and remain under the authority of the Spanish Government, shall be compelled to render any military service before peace be established over the whole territory.

Art. V.—Every individual, who by virtue of this capitulation may wish to depart from the Island, shall be permitted to do so, and the Spanish Government shall provide him with the means therefor, without passing through any town or settlement, if he so desires.

Art. VI.—The capitulation of each force shall take place in some uninhabited spot, where the arms and other munitions of war shall be previously deposited.

Art. VII.—In order to further the acceptance by the insurgents of the other departments of these articles of capitulation, the Commander-in-chief of the Spanish Army shall furnish them free transportation by land or sea, over all the lines within his control, to the Central Department.

Art. VIII.—This pact of the committee of the Central Department shall be deemed to have been made with all the departments of the Island which may accept its conditions.

Encampment of St. Augustin, February 10, 1878.

RAFAEL RODRIGUEZ, Secretary. E. L. LUACES.

As the liberties enjoyed by Porto Rico were very limited, the suffrage having been taken from it, and the powers of the Provincial Assembly and of the municipalities having been restricted, the liberties on the enjoyment of which Cuba could enter, in virtue of this treaty, were very few.

III.

The war being terminated, in virtue of the pact referred to, in 1878, political parties were organized.

The majority of the Peninsular Spaniards united to form the "Union Constitucional" party, whose platform was based on "unification" as a form of government; that is to say, the same laws and administrative methods for the Antilles as for Spain. In practice this party had been retrogressive; opposed systematically to all political reform, and always aiming at supremacy over the Spanish authorities. But it has been seen that a policy of suspicion and dislike toward the Cubans is not the one most conducive to the maintenance of peace, and, in reality, this policy has done more to prejudice the Spanish cause than all the secessionists and anti-Spaniards ever known.

In opposition to this party the Autonomist party was formed, composed of the Cubans who were opposed to the revolution that had just terminated, or who had belonged to it.

These parties were antagonistic, rather because of the accumulated resentment and suspicion engendered by the ten years' war than because of abstract principles, and the Autonomists had to enter on a titanic struggle to counteract the policy of the Conservative party and to maintain a direct intervention in the politics of the country.

This struggle was a hard one, not only because of the partiality almost invariably shown—up to three years ago —by the Government in Madrid to the Conservative party, but also because of the lack of civic qualities in the generality of the Cuban people, who have neither the education nor the character necessary to obtain by diplomatic means the liberties which they desire.

The separatists, who are unaware of their own defects, and who forget those of their countrymen when they bring charges against Spain, will be indignant with the Cuban who says this, but it is nevertheless the exact truth.

Educated abroad, outside the atmosphere of Cuban politics, when I returned to the Antilles I was able to study the political and social life of the Cubans and Porto Ricans, as well as the colonial policy of Spain, unbiased by prejudice; and I have invariably observed that for the evils of which my countrymen complain, and for which they blame the Government, they are themselves in a large measure responsible.

The Cuban people, like every other people that has not been educated to use its rights and that is ignorant of its duties, has always supposed that it was the mission of the Government to confer upon the people the liberties which they desire, without waiting even to be asked for them; and thus it has in general remained almost indifferent to the most important acts of modern politics; often, through a base self-interest, using its political rights in a manner opposed to its own convictions.

The "Union Constitucional" party has sent many Deputies to Madrid to work against the concession to Cuba of the liberties asked by her, supported by the suffrage of many Cubans who gave their votes through mercenary considerations and against their own feelings. I do not say opinions, because the nameless masses who vote for the sake of voting, in Cuba the same as in the United States and everywhere else, have no political convictions.

Owing to this lack of consistency the Autonomist party had to struggle both against the opposition of the Government and the intrigues of the opposite party, while it was at the same time badly seconded by the Cubans themselves, who were most deeply interested in the spread of the political doctrines of the party. The fact also that the Autonomist party had taken no share in the national party politics was highly prejudicial to it, for, as a result, none of the political parties of Spain had any interest in the triumph of the Autonomist Deputies.

An attitude of political unity with some one of the liberal national parties would undoubtedly have been highly favorable to the establishment of the reforms, and even of autonomy, in the Island.

Notwithstanding all these difficulties and drawbacks in the way of a really practical policy, since the conclusion of the peace of Zanjón (1878), which was obtained without compromising liberties already enjoyed (since Porto Rico had lost them in 1874), down to 1895, the following reforms were obtained:

Abolition of slavery.

Promulgation of the Constitution in force in Spain, by which the people of Cuba enjoy the same rights, whatever may have been the place of their birth, as those in the Peninsular Provinces.

The insurgent propagandists and their North American sympathizers have often asserted that the Cubans have neither inviolability of the domicile nor freedom of locomotion, nor of the press, nor of speech, and so on. All this is absolutely untrue.

Until a year ago, when the insurrection broke out, the country was occupied by a military force, as was natural and is the case in every country; all the liberties enjoyed in Spain were enjoyed there—the same liberties, social and political, as are enjoyed by the French, the Belgians, the Germans, &c.

By virtue of this Constitution no Cuban may be imprisoned except on the order of a judge, the accused being either indicted or set at liberty within seventy-two hours after his arrest.

Every Cuban has the right:

To express freely his views and opinions, orally or in writing, without being subject to the official censorship which existed up to the time of the promulgation of this law.

Thus in Cuba, as a proof that the exercise of this right is enjoyed, separatist newspapers and reviews supporting and defending the platform of Cuban independence have been published; as, for example, the separatist newspaper *La Protesta*, of Havana; the review *Hojas Literarias*, which was published up to January, 1895, and which was devoted to the separatist propaganda, and others.

Another equally false charge which has been made is that concerning freedom of locomotion: "No freedom of locomotion," and the pamphleteer adds: "No man, woman or child can travel from home unless provided with a license costing annually from 25 cents to $50; otherwise he is arrested; even beggars are not exempt from this tax."

If it were not because there are many simple-minded people who believe this sort of fairy tales I should not have mentioned this absurd statement, with which it is sought to influence the public mind, counting on the ignorance and credulity of the majority.

In Spain, the same as in other European countries, the identification of the individual is facilitated by means of a document signed by the Mayor or local authority, containing the personal description or affiliation of the person concerned, together with his signature. This document was presented in cases in which doubt might arise regarding the identity of the individual; as, for example, in collecting a debt, obtaining letters directed "poste restante," and in all legal matters. This document became subject to a tax, and then its presentation was required in all civil and political acts; but the document is not extended to minors, and the quota is so small (a workman pays 25 cents, a professional man, a physician, lawyer, &c., $2 annually) that it will be at once seen is no very great pecuniary sacrifice.

As for the assertion that no one can travel without this document, it is absurd; precisely because it is required only on rare occasions no one carries it about with him. I have traveled alone a great deal, both on horseback and in a carriage, and no official has ever asked for this document, nor could I have been arrested for not carrying it, as this is specially provided against by a Royal Decree relating to personal certificates, as they are called.

To continue the enumeration of the rights acquired since 1878:

The right of association.

Of assembly and of holding political or other meetings.

The electoral right was also obtained, this privilege having been extended to every taxpayer whose taxes amount to $5 annually, the various sources from which such taxes are derived being cumulative.*

Provincial Assemblies were organized for the inspection of municipal accounts, charities and public works of a secondary character. It is true that these assemblies have given only a negative result, owing to their having been established under the same conditions as exist in the Peninsula; but this failure has only shown how impracticable the unification theory is in certain cases, and has fully justified the advocates of decentralization, particularly for the Island of Cuba.

A municipal law was also promulgated for the creation of municipalities.

The tribunals of justice, classified as Inferior (municipal), Superior and Supreme Courts, are sufficiently well distributed for the satisfactory administration of justice.

The same Civil Law in force in the Peninsula was proclaimed.

The same Commercial Code and Law of Mortgages.

Registry and Civil Marriage.

---

* See page 78.

The same Penal Laws as obtain in the Peninsula.

In regard to higher public education, liberty of instruction was proclaimed, by virtue of which studies may be conducted privately, it being sufficient to take the regular college examinations to receive a Degree.

Here, briefly outlined, are the principal reforms obtained by Cuba, and which practically placed the Cuban people in possession of all the rights attached to Spanish citizenship.

If it be true that the genuinely Cuban representation in Congress has been but scant, and Cuban intervention in the provincial and municipal administration only limited, this is not owing alone to the partiality of the Government for the Conservatives, but is also due to the little civic spirit shown by the majority of the people in making use of their rights. In those districts where the majority of the people have manifested greater interest and enthusiasm in using their political rights the Autonomists have had a majority in the municipalities and in the Provincial Assemblies, and have sent their Deputies to the Cortes.

For example:

The representation in the Cortes of the Province of Puerto Principe has always been Autonomist since 1879.

Half of the representation of the Province of Santiago de Cuba, and also of Santa Clara, has been Autonomist.

The Provincial Assemblies of Santa Clara, Santiago de Cuba and Puerto Principe have had a Liberal majority, and many town councils (as that of Sancti Spiritus), have been almost entirely Autonomist.

The following is the platform of the Cuban Liberal or Autonomist party, organized August 9, 1878, six months after the conclusion of the treaty of Zanjón:

Social Question.

The exact fulfillment of Article 21 of the Moret Law, in its first clause, which says: "The Government shall lay before the Cortes, as soon as the Cuban Deputies shall have been admitted into it, the plan of a law of indemnified emancipation of those who may remain in slavery after the promulgation of this law." Simultaneous regulation of free colored labor, and the moral and intellectual instruction of the freedman.

White immigration exclusively, preference being given to that of families, and the removal of all obstacles in the way of Peninsular and foreign immigration; both to be undertaken privately.

POLITICAL QUESTION.

Necessary Liberties.—Extension of individual rights guaranteed by Title 1 of the Constitution: to wit, freedom of the press, of meeting and of association. Right of petition. Also, freedom of religion and of instruction, orally and in books.

Admission of Cubans, equally with other Spaniards, to all public offices and employments, in accordance with Article 15 of the Constitution,

Integral application of the municipal, electoral and other organic laws of the Peninsula to the Islands of Cuba and Porto Rico, without any other changes than those demanded by local needs or interests, in accordance with the *spirit* of the pact of Zanjón.

Fulfillment of Article 89 of the Constitution; the particular system of Spanish laws being understood, which shall favor the greatest decentralization possible within the national unity.

Separation and independence of the civil and military powers.

Application to Cuba of the Penal Code, of the Law of Criminal Procedure, of the Law of Mortgages, of that of the Administration of Justice, of the most recent Commercial Code, and other legislative reforms, with such modifications as may be demanded by local interests.

ECONOMIC QUESTION.

Abolishment of export duties on all the products of the Island.

Reformation of the Cuban tariff in the sense that import duties shall be purely fiscal; those having the character of *differential* duties, whether *specific* or of the *flag*, being abolished.

Reduction of the duties paid in the custom houses of the Peninsula on Cuban sugar and molasses to the rate of *fiscal* duties.

Treaties of commerce between Spain and other countries, particularly the United States, on the basis of the most complete reciprocity of the tariff between them and Cuba, the same exemption from taxes and the same privileges being conceded to the products of other countries in the custom houses and ports of the Island as they concede to our products in theirs.

HAVANA, August 1, 1878.

This important document was signed by José Maria Galvez, Juan Esportuno, Carlos Saladrigas, Francisco P. Gay, Miguel Bravo y Sentís, Ricardo del Monte, Juan Bruno Zayas, José Eugenio Bernal, Joaquin G. Lebredo, Pedro Armenteros y del Castillo, Emilio I. Lucas, Antonio Govín and Manuel Pérez de Molina, editor of *El Triunfo.*

With this platform the Autonomist party began a double political campaign, in the mother country and in Cuba, with the result that in 1893 a Minister of the Crown, Señor Maura, presented to the Cortes a plan of administrative reforms which constituted a radical change in the manner of governing the Antilles and which was the first important step in political evolution toward colonial autonomy; and in Cuba the majority of the Peninsular Spaniards separated from the uncompromising party called Conservative, and formed another liberal party with the name of Reformist, which presented the following platform:

PLATFORM OF THE REFORMIST PARTY.

POLITICAL QUESTION.

Faithful and exact observance of the National Constitution, which recognizes and guarantees individual rights and proclaims the necessity of the transatlantic provinces being governed by special laws, without prejudice to the authority which it confers upon the Government to apply to the same the laws promulgated for the Peninsula, with such modifications as it may deem expedient, holding itself responsible to the Cortes therefor.

Application to the Island of all the laws made, or which may be made, in the Peninsula, to insure mutual respect for the rights recognized by title of the Constitution, and of the organic laws, without any other modification than those which may be indispensably required by the genius or the customs of the people, subject to the before-mentioned criterion of special legislation.

Extension of the right to elect Deputies to the Cortes, Provincial Assemblymen and Councilors to all Spaniards born and residing in Cuba, as the conditions of the Island may counsel and demand, and in correspondence with the institutions which in this respect obtain in the Peninsula.

Approbation and immediate promulgation of the law laid before the Chamber of Deputies on the 5th day of last June, for the government and civil administration of this Island and of Porto Rico.

Without prejudice to the reforms which the new provincial organization may in the future demand, and which experience may advise, the Assembly shall have, among other powers, that of approving the accounts of the municipalities; the revision and interpretation of the resolutions of those bodies which do not come within the exclusive jurisdiction of the same, and other matters of local administration; the right of appointing and removing all their functionaries and clerks; jurisdiction in everything relating to the administration and encouragement of the moral and material interests of the Island, without prejudice to the powers of the Town Councils, General Government or Supreme Government; the power of issuing decrees of a general and obligatory character for the whole of the Island in regard to public instruction, public works, establishment of banks and partnerships, the making of loans and other similar matters; that of discussing and proposing to the General Government and the Supreme Government, when the case arises, whatever it may deem expedient for the interests of the Island, and which is not within their jurisdiction; that of reporting on the imposition of new taxes, changes in existing taxes and other measures of a financial character; and that of proposing to the General Government the creation, change or abolishment of any local impost.

Constitution of the General Council of Administration, with the powers conceded to it by the plan of reforms of Señor Maura, that part of it relating to the electoral right being especially emphasized.

Law determining the powers of the Governor General of the Island, his responsibilities, the rank and personal qualifications necessary for his appointment, no class of the State being excluded.

Law relating to public employees, authorizing the entrance into the civil professions only of those Spaniards settled in Cuba, without distinction of origin, who shall have the necessary qualifications therefor, reserving to the Supreme Government the appointment of chiefs of departments and chiefs of the provincial officers, the remaining appointments being made by the Governor General.

Examination and revision of the accounts pertaining to the Budget of the Island in such manner as to expedite their settlement by the Bureau of Local Administration.

ECONOMIC QUESTION.

Reorganization of the departments and of the administration and reduction of the public expenditures.

Immediate abolition of the Law of Commercial Relations, until such time as free trade shall be established with the Peninsula.

Reform of the tariff, until a purely fiscal tariff is reached, without prejudice to the legitimate needs of the Treasury; and reform also of the custom house laws and the tariff commission.

Abolition of the duty on exports.

Celebration of special commercial treaties which shall regulate the relations of this Island with foreign countries.

Revision of existing treaties, especially of that made with the United States, in order to obtain favorable conditions for the exportation of tobacco and free it from the disadvantages under which it labors.

Free sale of tobacco in the Peninsula after the corresponding duties have been paid.

Total abolishment of all taxes on manufactured tobacco.

Abolishment of the present industrial tax on sugar.

Law to organize agricultural credit on terms favorable to the encouragement of agriculture, and reform of the Law of Civil Procedure fór the benefit of farms held in partnership, in order to facilitate the speedy and economical division and inscription of the same.

Definitive liquidation of the public debt and such readjustment thereof as shall diminish its interest and insure the reduction to an annual amount compatible with the public revenues and the needs of the country.

Creation of a well ordered monetary system.

Revision by a special court, and within a limited period, of the documents of classification of pensioners, and a new method of payment of the same which, while respecting acquired rights, shall at the same time permit of an alleviation of this annual charge upon the Budget.

HAVANA, October 30, 1893.

The intrigues of the remainder of the uncompromising Spanish party of Cuba, who combated in Congress the plan of reforms, resulted in delaying the passage of the Law of Reforms for the Antilles until February, 1895, and then in introducing changes which, although unimportant, caused dissatisfaction to both of the Liberal Cuban parties.

But the very fact of this plan of reforms having been under discussion for two years proves that if the Autonomist party had united with the Liberal party of the Peninsula, the latter would have taken a more active interest in the adoption of the reforms, and they would have become a law, in opposition to the wishes of the Conservatives, long before they did, and probably without the changes made in them posteriorly.

So that, to repeat what I have already said, in the same way as the lack of public spirit of many of the Cuban electors in neglecting to make an opportune use of their political rights, or in using them to the prejudice of their country for mercenary or selfish ends, prevented, on many occasions, liberal Cubans from being elected Deputies to the Spanish Cortes, so did the lack of political knowledge or judgment of some of the leaders of the Autonomist party in desiring to be exclusively *regionists* deprive them of the assured support of any of the national parties.

IV.

Having reviewed the political movement of Cuba, I will now describe briefly its state of culture, and then proceed to show the stage of material progress to which it has attained, comparing this, for the better appreciation of the facts, with that of the sister countries throughout the continent which are to-day independent states.

The civilization of the Cuban people had its origin, as I have already said—adducing in support of the statement the authoritative testimony of a distinguished American writer, Mr. A. R. Marshall—in the ancient Laws of the Indies, which carried to America all the science, arts and literature of Spain, establishing a current sympathy and constant interchange in the sphere of intellectual speculation among all the Spanish speaking peoples.

For this reason it is that, as is constantly observed, all the South Americans are familiar with the domestic habits of the Spanish people; that when they go to Spain, whether they visit the great cities or the smallest villages of the various provinces or districts, in each of which the usages, customs and even the dialect of the people are different, they always find themselves familiar with that particular manner of life, because American civilization is in reality a compound of the heterogeneous elements of Iberian civilization characterized by the marks of its adaptation to a different environment, and having also its own proper characteristics, which are more or less distinctly marked in American civilization, according to the influence, that is to say the grade, of civilization of the conquered peoples.

For this reason, while in Mexico and Peru European civilization is strongly marked by the traits of Aztec and Inca civilization, respectively, which were noteworthy, in the Antilles, where the aboriginal races had reached only a very rudimentary stage of civillzation, the typical characteristics of Indian life are now only observable in the name of some place or in the origin or foundation of some custom which is gradually dying out.

On the other hand, the Peninsular Spaniards who emigrate to Spanish America find themselves in a social environment so exactly resembling their own that, except for the physical acclimatization, they scarcely feel the change; they adapt themselves insensibly to the new environment, with the result that after a few years they become members of the Spanish-American family, a thing which takes place with no other European emigrants.

In Cuba and Porto Rico the grade of general culture is undoubtedly higher than in any other part of Spanish America, because, in addition to the fact that contact with exterior culture is facilitated by the extent of their coast line relatively to the area of the country, it has also been favored by the admirable qualifications of the greater part of the people for the assimilation of progressive ideas.

The difference which I have noticed has also been caused in part by the circumstance that while on the continent occupations of a political character absorbed from the beginning of the century the majority of the able minds that might have employed themselves usefully in other elevated intellectual pursuits, many men of ability living on the continent, and disinclined for the disturbed and dangerous existence on which those countries were entering, emigrated to Cuba and Porto Rico.

In a short work like the present it would be impossible even to mention the names of all the notable men who, born in Cuba or outside of it, have contributed in the present century to the progress of the Island, I will endeavor, however, to notice briefly the most noteworthy, in order to give an idea of this manifestation of the culture of the country.

I will mention the reverend professor, Father Varela, who introduced modern philosophy into the schools of Cuba and who educated many Cubans who have done honor to their country.

Prof. José de la Luz Caballero, of Havana, a professor at the age of twenty-four, the translator of Volney and a member of the Royal Economic Academy of Florence, author of various works, vice-director of the Patriotic Society, admitted to the bar in 1836, a member of the Academy of Letters of Barcelona, &c.

Francisco Arango y Parreño, of Havana, admitted to the bar at the age of twenty-five, he went to Spain as the agent of the Municipality of Havana. He obtained the administrative reforms of 1789–94. He was commissioned by Count Montalvo to make a scientific journey through France and England in 1793. He introduced into Cuba the cultivation of sugar cane of Tahiti, and published various works on agriculture and commerce and some books of travels. In 1815 he crowned his labors by obtaining from the mother country, in spite of the opposition of the monopolists, the right of free trade for the ports of Cuba, which changed completely the manner of life of the colony. Baron Humboldt mentions him with encomium in his works. The Spanish Government rewarded his labors for his country's welfare, conferring upon him the title of Grandee of the Kingdom.

In all his patriotic enterprises he was supported by Governor General Luis de las Casas, whose name ought also to figure among those of the men who have most contributed to the progress of the Island.

José Silverio Jorrin, of Havana, a lawyer by profession, and a magistrate of the courts of Havana and of Burgos, in Spain; author of various works on history, mathematics, political economy and pedagogy; translator of Tacitus; Deputy to the Cortes and member of various scientific societies, among others the Historical Society of New York.

José Antonio Saco, of Bayamo, a distinguished statesman, Deputy to the Cortes several times, and later on a revolutionist, author of important works on history and social science.

Ramon de la Sagra, Director of the Botanical Garden of Havana, corresponding member of the Royal Institute of France, and author of Monumental, Physical and Political History of Cuba, which was translated into French in 1844.

General Francisco Albear y Lara, of Havana, a professor in the School of Engineers of Guadalajara (Spain) in

1842 at twenty-six years of age, and sub-inspector of the School of Engineers in his own country at twenty-eight. He died six years ago, after having superintended the construction of the aqueduct of Havana, for the plan of which he received a prize at the Paris Exposition in 1878.

Felipe Poey, an eminent naturalist, who for his works on the Cuban flora and fauna was elected corresponding member of the Zoölogical Society of London and the Entomological Society of France. It may be added that the savants, Cuvier and Valenciennes, mention him in their works as the naturalist who has contributed most to the knowledge of the natural history of the Antilles. His great work, "Cuban Icthyology," was purchased by the Spanish Government.

As it would be impossible to enumerate the merits of all the Cubans who have distinguished themselves, I will notice briefly a few others only.

As eminent statesmen and political economists, prior to the revolution of 1868: The Count of Pozos Dulces; F. T. Rodriguez, a lawyer by profession, and also a professor in the University of Havana; G. de Navarrete, Rector of the Almshouse; F. T. Balmaceda, who emigrated to New Granada, and who was appointed by that Government its Minister to Madrid; Calixto Bernal, Portuondo, Millet, Deputies to Cortes; José Guell y Renté, a Senator of the Kingdom for the University of Havana, who, while in Spain, married a Princess who was a sister of the King, Don Francisco de Asis, and a cousin of Queen Isabella II.; J. R. Betancourt, Deputy; Thomas Gener, an illustrious Catalan, and Carlos Rodriguez Batista, who was Civil Governor of Havana.

Among contemporaries I will mention the most noteworthy of those whose names occur to me: R. M. de Labra, a lawyer by profession, a Senator of the Kingdom and an eminent statistician and pedagogue; Gálvez, the present President of the Autonomist party; G. Saladrigas, ex-President of the Provincial Assembly and an Autonomist; A. Govín, also an Autonomist and a distinguished lawyer; N. Azcárate, an eminent statesman of the Spanish Republican party; R. Fernandez de Castro, an Autonomist Deputy and Commissioner in Madrid of the Planters' Club; E. Terry, Figueroa, Eliseo Giberga, R. Montoro, all Deputies and distinguished orators; Suarez Bruzon and Conté, Peninsulars and both Autonomists. The Spanish Generals, Serrano and Dulce, whose names, as her Governors, Cuba remembers with affection, have also contributed to the cultivation and propagation of modern ideas.

Among university professors and teachers: Escobedo, Deputy to Cortes in 1836; A. Guiteras, the translator of Virgil; J. Fornaris, Nicolás Guiteras, Rector of the University of Havana, founder of the Academy of Sciences of New Orleans, and Vice-President of the Medical Congress of Washington, and many others; for the majority of the professors, past and present, of the university, were born in Cuba, as was the present Rector of the University, Dr. Joaquin Lastres.

Distinguished engineers, in addition to Albear, already mentioned: Menocal, of the United States Navy, author of a plan of a canal for Nicaragua; and Portuondo, colonel of engineers, professor of mathematics, author of a treatise on architecture which is used at the present time as a text book in Spain, and Autonomist Deputy to Cortes.

Eminent naturalists: José Velaro y Diaz and Carlos de la Torre, the latter appointed a professor in the University of Havana at the age of twenty-four, after passing a competitive examination in Madrid.

Writers on agriculture: Antonio Bachiller y Morales; J. F. Balmaceda, Alvaro Reinoso, Zayas, &c. Among those who have most contributed to the encouragement of Cuban agriculture may be mentioned the philanthropist, the Count of Casa Moré, of Colombia, who settled at an early age in Cuba, and there amassed a fortune, which he devoted to the establishment of a practical school of agriculture, on which he expended over $200,000.

Among the philanthropists of Cuba I will mention the Abreu family of Santa Clara. One member of this family, Doña Marta Abreu de Estevez, married to a professor of the University of Havana, Dr. Luis Estevez, also a Cuban, maintains public schools, a dispensary and an almshouse; she has constructed public lavatories for the poor, a beautiful theatre and an electric plant for lighting the city.

Terry, the father of the present Autonomist Deputy of the same name, bequeathed to the city of Cienfuegos a sum of money for the erection of a theatre, the construction of which was undertaken by his son, and which is now one of the most beautiful in Latin America. The proceeds of the theatre are devoted to the support of public schools.

Among the poets and artists, of whom there have been many, the following are most generally known: Gertrudis Gómez de Avellaneda; Heredia, author of the famous Ode to Niagara; Plácido, Zenea, Luaces, Navarrete and others; the violinists, Albertini and White, both of whom took first prizes in the Paris Conservatoire; Espadero, pianist and composer, who was the intimate friend of Gottschalk, Cervantes, Brindis de Salas and others.

In conclusion, I will mention the names of some other distinguished Cubans, who, although they have not devoted themselves exclusively to the advancement of their country, are yet brilliant ornaments to her, and prove how easy it would have been for the Cubans to make themselves prominent in the Peninsula: Señor Abarzuza, Minister of the Colonies in the last Liberal Cabinet; Osma, the present Under Secretary of that department; Francisco Lastres, Vice-President of the Chamber of Deputies and a lawyer of distinction. The present Minister of War,

General Azcárraga, has already been mentioned, but this illustrious soldier was born in the Philippine Islands.

General Arderius, however, who was Governor of Havana in the time of General Martinez Campos, General Gonzales Muñoz, Loño, Rodriguez, Barzon, Bosch, Garrich, Godoy, Zarco del Valle, Genaro de Quesada, De Ezpeleta, Ampudia, Felix Ferrer and Francisco Acosta are all Cubans.

When a country with hardly a million and a half of inhabitants has produced in such abundance intellect of so high an order and as varied as distinguished, it must be acknowledged that the civilizing spirit of its colonizers has been notable and beneficial; and that we may be justly proud of being Spaniards, although we may have had more or less difficulty in realizing our political ideals; for, after all, the mother country also has had her political ideals, as all the peoples of the earth have had and will always have theirs.

V.

From the beginning to the middle of the present century the population of Cuba increased but little, the increase being estimated at 600,000 inhabitants, or an average of 4 per cent. annually. Of the total population in 1841 (1,007,684) 600,000 were colored, a third being free and the remainder slaves.

Comparing the figures with those of the Census of 1846, which showed a colored population of 473,000 souls (more than half the population of the Island), of which 150,000 were free, it is noticeable that, while the population as a whole increased, the colored population diminished, and the proportion of the slave population to the free diminished also.

This increase in the white population, with a simultaneous decrease in the colored, has continued, repeating itself in each succeeding census, as a consequence of the process which foreigners of every country must undergo, whose constitution does not readily adapt itself to their new environment.

According to the Census of 1877, the Island had a population of 1,620,000. The increase in the sixteen years which had elapsed from 1861 was barely an average of 1 per cent. annually, notwithstanding the long period of civil war through which the Island had been passing since 1868. As for the colored population, it reached a total of barely 538,000, or 33 per cent. of the total population.

Finally, the last census (1887), gives a total of 1,681,000 inhabitants, only 528,000 being colored, 30.6 per cent. of the whole population. So that for each 694 whites there were only 306 of the colored race, between negroes and mulattoes, the increase in the population during the decade being 1.65 per cent. annually.

Taking these figures as a basis, I think it may be safely assumed that the population of the Island at the breaking out of the present insurrection—eight years having passed since the publication of the last census and taking the average increase which the above numbers show—was not more than 2,100,000, nor the colored population more than 520,000, or 25 per cent. of that number; that is to say, 750 whites to 250 negroes, mulattoes and Chinese. These last, according to the Census of 1887, amounted only to 43,811 in the whole Island, and since that time the number has decreased considerably.

Comparing these data with the same data in relation to the Spanish-American republics we shall have the following proportion for the sixty years between 1825–85:

Country.	Pop. in 1825-30.	Pop. in 1885-90.	Per Cent. of increase in 60 years.
1. Argentine Republic,	720,000	4,066,000	406
2. Porto Rico,	200,000	800,000	300
3. Uruguay,	214,000	706,000	230
4. CUBA,	703,000	1,681,000	140
5. Bolivia,	1,090,000	2,333,000	114
6. Central America,	1,700,000	3,121,000	084
7. Peru,	1,500,000	2,621,000	075
8. Chili,	1,650,000	2,817,000	070

	COUNTRY.	Pop. in 1825-30.	Pop. in 1885-90.	Per Cent. of increase in 60 years.
	Colombia (to-day),	......	4,000,000	..
9.	Ecuador,	......	1,272,000	068
	Venezuela,	......	2,323,000	..
10.	Mexico,	7,200,000	11,630,000	067
11.	Paraguay,	200,000	329,000	060
	Hayti and Santo Domingo,	936,000	......	
	Hayti,	......	572,000	..
	Santo Domingo,	......	400,000	004

As will be seen, next to the Argentine Republic, whose increase in population has been considered phenomenal, ranks the Island of Porto Rico, which is relatively almost as thickly populated as Germany, and more so than France. Next comes Uruguay, in which the conditions are very similar to those in the Argentine Republic, and then Cuba; none of the other republics have increased as much in population as the Spanish Antilles; and in the Island of Santo Domingo, in which the black race predominates, the increase in sixty years has been only 4 per cent.

The following diagram shows the progressive increase of the population of Cuba, with corresponding percentage as to color:

POPULATION OF CUBA.

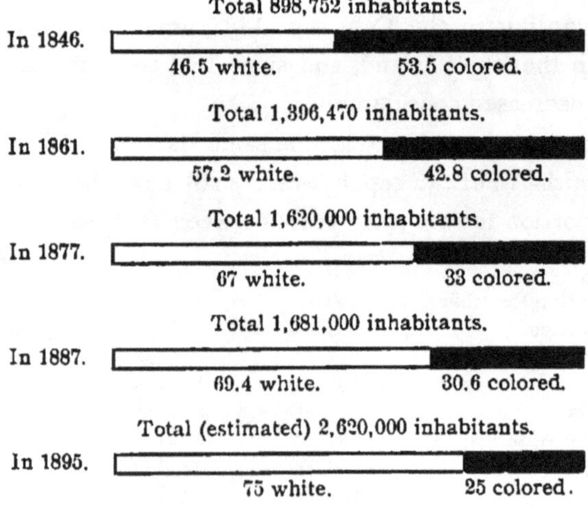

For the figures which follow we shall take as authority the Census of 1887, which is the last official census published.

The population of the six provinces into which Cuba is now divided is as follows:

	Inhabitants.	To Square Kil.	To Square Mile.
Havana,	481,928	56	20
Matanzas,	359,578	42	15
Pinar del Rio,	225,891	15	5½
Puerto Principe,	67,789	02.1	0.7
Santa Clara,	374,122	20.5	7.4
Santiago de Cuba,	273,379	7.8	2.8

As will be seen, the two most thickly populated provinces are Matanzas and Havana, the population of each of which is relatively greater than that of some European states.

The province which has the largest colored population is Matanzas, the proportion being forty-five blacks to fifty-five whites; next comes Santiago de Cuba, with forty blacks to sixty whites; that which has the least being Puerto Principe, with twenty blacks to eighty whites.

Of the white population of the Island more than a third can read and write, while of the colored race only 12 per cent. have attained this degree of intellectual culture. The provinces in which the highest grade of education exists are Havana and Puerto Principe, in which for every 100 inhabitants forty-seven and forty-four among the whites, and fifteen and twenty-eight among the blacks, respectively, can read and write. The most backward is Pinar del Rio, in which only seventeen whites and three negroes in each 100 inhabitants can read and write. It is for this reason, and not because the Ethiopian race abounds there more than in other provinces, that this province is called in Cuba "the black continent."

In none of the Spanish-American Republics does the number of inhabitants who can read and write reach 35 per cent.

Passing on to classify the population of the Island in urban and rural, we shall have the following figures:

TOWNS OF MORE THAN 10,000 INHABITANTS.

Havana,	220,000	Sancti-Spiritu,	15.000
Puerto Principe,	41,000	Sagua la Grande,	12,000
Santiago de Cuba,	40,000	Guines,	11,000
Matanzas,	38,000	Trinidad,	11,000
Cienfuegos,	25,000	Regla,	10,300
Guanabacoa,	23,000	San Antonio de los Baños,	10,000
Cardenas,	20,700	Remedios,	10,000
Santa Clara,	16,000	Manzanillo,	16,000

TOWNS OF FROM 2,000 TO 10,000 INHABITANTS.

PROVINCE OF HAVANA.

Alquizar,	2,000	Marianao,	5,500
Bejucal,	5,300	Madruga,	3,500
Cano,	2,000	San José de las Lajas,	3,100
Guira de Melena,	2,500	Santiago de las Vegas,	5,000
Jaruco,	2,500	Vereda Nueva,	2,000

PROVINCE OF MATANZAS.

Bolondron,	2,100	Palmillas,	2,800
Colon,	5,900	Roque,	2,000
Corral Falso,	3,200	Sabanilla,	3,000
Jovellanos,	5,000	Union de Reyes,	4,100

PROVINCE OF PINAR DEL RIO.

Consolación Sur,	2,000	Pinar del Rio,	6,500
Guanajay,	5,500	San Juan Martinez,	2,600

PROVINCE OF SANTA CLARA.

Abrens,	3,000	Placetas,	4,500
Caibarien,	4,000	Palmira,	4,500
Cartagena,	2,000	Santo Domingo,	2,800
Camajuani,	2,500	Santa Isabel,	2,500
Esperanza,	4,000	San Juan Teras,	2,300

PROVINCE OF SANTIAGO DE CUBA.

Alto del Songo,	2,500	Gibara,	8,600
Bayamo,	7,800	Guantanamo,	7,300
Baracoa,	4,900	Holguin,	7,500
Cobre,	5,000	Victoria Tunas,	4,555

PROVINCE OF PUERTO PRINCIPE.

Ciego de Avila,	3,000	Nuevitas,	4,900
Moron,	4,000		

Taking the above figures with the total population of each province, we can form the following diagram, by means of which we can estimate at a glance the proportion that exists between the urban and the rural population:

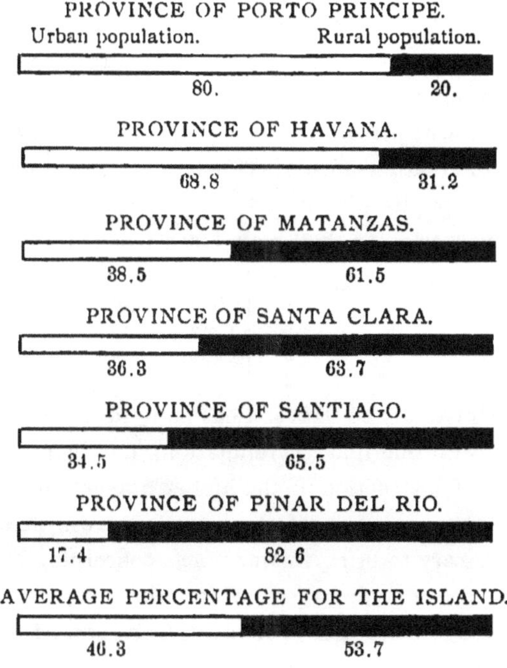

Calculating that in the towns of less than 10,000 inhabitants half of the able-bodied male population is employed in agricultural labors or in occupations connected with agriculture, we shall have a rural population of 1,000,000 of inhabitants out of the total population of 1,680,000, which signifies that over 250,000 men between the ages of eighteen and sixty are employed in the labors of the field.

If primary instruction is not so widely diffused in Cuba as could be desired, the causes for it may be found in the prejudices of the authorities and the lack of good methods of teaching, and also in the fact that the heads of families among the rural working classes manifest in general but little disposition to send their children to school, in some cases through ignorance and in others from a selfish desire to avail themselves of their children's assistance in their labors.

Taking these circumstances into consideration the fact that 35 per cent. of the population can read and write is very consoling.

There are at present in Cuba over 1,200 primary schools, with a total attendance of 83,000 pupils ; comparing the number of pupils who attend school with that of the following countries we shall have for:

	Per Cent.		Per Cent.
Uruguay,	8	Venezuela,	4.5
Argentine Republic,	6	Chili,	4.1
CUBA,	5	Brazil,	2.1
Mexico,	4.7		

The University of Havana has enjoyed for many years past so well merited a reputation, and her advanced methods of instruction in the higher branches of learning and in the professions are so generally known, that I deem it unnecessary to bring forward facts concerning her.

In the field of journalism, which also serves to indicate the degree of culture of a country, Cuba has no reason to envy any Latin-American State.

In Cuba 170 periodicals were published last year; Havana, with a population of 220,000, had twenty dailies, almost all of them advocates of some political doctrine, from the support of the old colonial rule to that of the separatist propaganda, the discussion of the latter question by word and pen having been authorized by a special Decree of the Supreme Court of Madrid. The same city has also forty-four semi-weekly and weekly and twenty-eight fortnightly and monthly periodicals, being a total of ninety-two publications, including political, technological and literary.

The City of Mexico, with a population of 340,000, has almost the same number of periodicals as Havana (ninety-six), twenty of which also are dailies.

Buenos Ayres, with three times the population of Havana, has only 161 periodicals.

Caracas has a greater number of periodicals than Havana or than any other Spanish-American city, having forty-four publications for a population of 80,000. But Venezuela, taken as a whole, has fewer than Cuba.

Comparing Cuba with each of the principal South American republics, in the number of inhabitants to each publication issued in it, we have the following:

CUBA,	1 per each		9,050
Uruguay,	1	" "	11,000
Venezuela,	1	" "	24,000
Mexico,	1	" "	28,000
Chili,	1	" "	41,000
Argentine Republic,	1	" "	49,000

In concluding this sketch of the data, which indicates the degree of a country's culture, I will mention briefly the scientific and charitable corporations and establishments in Havana, omitting those which are under the exclusive control of the State:

Academy of Medical Sciences.

Academy of Sciences and Letters.

Dental Academy.

Seven asylums for orphans, the aged and the poor.

Three public libraries, besides those of various societies, which are open to the public.

Four banks—the Spanish Bank, the Spanish Colonial Bank, the Bank of Commerce and the Agricultural Bank, besides various savings banks.

The Spanish Club.

Consultative centres, called "colleges" of notaries, dentists, notaries public and attorneys.

Three companies for supplying light to the city—two gas companies and one electric light company.

A Conservatory of Music.

High Schools, a Male Normal School and a Female Normal School, for the study of medicine; a Professional

School of Painting and Sculpture and two of Arts and Trades.

An Alms House, an Insane Asylum, and a School for Deaf Mutes.

Seven Hospitals, some of them constructed for the purpose according to the newest scientific methods.

Grammar schools in all the wards.

Institute of Vaccination.

Chemical and Histo-Bacteriological Laboratories, both private and municipal.

Registry of Intellectual Property. (Copyright.)

Economic Society of Friends of the Country, Anthropological Society, Society for the Protection of Children, Society for Clinical Studies, Odontological Society, and others.

Seven theatres, among them the well-known Tacon and Payret Theatres.

An Institute for the Treatment of Hydrophobia and seventy-one different societies for purposes of instruction, entertainment, charity and mutual aid.

The above facts will, I think, suffice to give a clear idea of the social and political condition of Cuba.

VI.

Cuba has at the present time a complete railroad system in the Provinces of Matanzas and Havana; a well developed system in those of Pinar del Rio and Santa Clara, and one sufficiently developed to connect the centres of population with the ports in those of Puerto Principe and Santiago de Cuba. All the material employed by the railroad companies is American, the locomotives being generally those manufactured by Baldwin, of Philadelphia, which make an average speed of 30 miles an hour.

The first railroad was established in Cuba in 1836—earlier than in many European countries, and not later than in any other country except Belgium and the United States. There are at present in operation, open to the public, 3,200 kilometres, or about 2,000 miles, of railroad, and an equal length devoted to private service connected with the public roads for the use of the sugar plantations. Among the Latin-American countries Cuba holds the first place in extent of railroads, in proportion to extent of territory, the third in their extent in proportion to population, and the fourth in actual extent.

The following table shows the length of the railroads in operation in South America:

	Miles.		Miles
Agentine Republic,	7,676	Colombia,	218
Mexico.	5,812	Costa Rica,	161
Brazil.	5,582	Porto Rico,	153
CUBA,	2,000	Paraguay,	152
Chili,	1,682	Salvador,	120
Uruguay,	991	Nicaragua,	90
Peru,	883	Honduras,	69
Guatemala,	460	Ecuador,	56
Venezuela,	282	Santo Domingo,	50

Porto Rico holds the twelfth place in the extent of her railroad system, but she holds a much higher place in general means of communication, as she has first-class highways, like those of Europe, which traverse the island from north to south, crossing the mountains at an altitude at some points of 2,200 feet above the level of the sea. These highways reach a total length of 140 miles, and were constructed by the Government. The Government also constructed, between the years 1860 and 1868, about 250 miles of road along the shore of the island; but when the municipalities were formed in 1869 those roads passed into the hands of the local corporations, which have unfortunately so entirely neglected them that at the present time they are in very much the same condition as the roads of Santo Domingo constructed by the Spanish, which neither during the Haytian rule nor under the republic received any care whatever.

In proportion to the density of the population there is for each 10,000 inhabitants the following extent of railroad:

	Miles.		Miles.
Argentine Republic, . .	18.8	Guatemala, ...	3.1
Uruguay, ...	14	Nicaragua, ...	2.8
CUBA, ...	12½	Ecuador, ...	2.2
Costa Rica, ...	6.6	Porto Rico, ...	1.9
Chili, ...	5.9	Honduras, ...	1.6
Mexico, ...	5	Salvador, ...	1.5
Paraguay, ...	4.6	Venezuela, ...	1.2
Peru, ...	3.4	Colombia, ...	0.5

And in regard to the most important particular, that is the length of the roads in proportion to the area of the country, which is what will give the clearest idea of its facilities for transportation, the following table will show the number of miles of surface:

	Lineal Miles.		Lineal Miles.
United States of America (North), ...	55.5	Chili, ...	5.8
CUBA, ...	57.	Guatemala, ...	4.4
Porto Rico, ...	42.	Peru, ...	1.9
Salvador, ...	17.1	Nicaragua, ...	1.9
Uruguay, ...	13.7	Brazil, ...	1.7
Mexico, ...	7.5	Honduras, ...	1.5
Costa Rica, ...	6.	Venezuela, ...	.5
Argentine Republic, .	6.8	Colombia, ...	.4
		Ecuador, ...	.2

I shall make no mention of the telegraphic lines, for I suppose there is no country in the world in which a bird could fly without danger of striking against telegraph wires, but I will speak of the postal and telegraphic movement, for this is a determining factor of a country's activity.

According to the figures of the Almanack de Gotha, of 1887 (for in later editions they are omitted), and of the official works published by the Bureau of American Republics, of Washington, of 1891–94, Cuba occupies the twenty-first and eighteenth places, respectively, in the use of the telegraph and the mails among the countries of the world, and the third place among the Latin-American countries, as the following statistics will show.

Statistics of correspondence received and sent in one year, per capita:

Uruguay,	21.8	Guatemala,	2.6
Chili,	12.3	Brazil,	2.5
CUBA,	11.4	Peru,	1.8
Mexico,	11.3	Ecuador,	1.5
Costa Rica,	8.9	Venezuela,	1.3
Argentine Republic,	8.	Honduras,	0.9
Nicaragua,	6.5	Paraguay,	0.6
Porto Rico,	4.		

Number of telegraphic dispatches for each 100 inhabitants received and sent:

Costa Rica,	30	Porto Rico,	11
Guatemala,	24	Colombia,	10
CUBA,	21	Venezuela,	8
Chili,	21	Peru,	4
Argentine Republic,	19	Brazil,	3
Uruguay,	13		

The wealth of the country has increased to such an extent that its amount per capita will bear comparison with that of the most prosperous countries of Europe, or with that of the United States. Its total value last year amounted to $850,000,000, or $531 per capita. In the United States the total amount was, in 1890, $25,473,000,000, or $407.18 per capita.

Compared with some of the States of the Union, Cuba would occupy twelfth place, as to the average capitation of wealth, according to the following showing:

	Per Capita.		Per Capita
Massachusetts,	$962	Utah,	$510
Rhode Island,	931	Maryland,	507
California,	911	Pennsylvania,	505
Montana,	854	Vermont,	487
New Hampshire,	698	Ohio,	484
District of Columbia,	665	North Dakota,	482
New York,	631	Connecticut,	480
Washington,	632	Arizona,	470
New Jersey,	618	Maine,	467
Nevada,	573	Minnesota,	452
Wyoming,	535	Michigan,	428
Colorado,	535	South Dakota,	426
Oregon,	529		

In the remaining States the wealth per capita is less than $400. (See the official statistics of the United States Government.)

The value of the rural real estate alone in Cuba, in 1887, was $220,902,900 gold, giving a rental of 17,000,000 annually, which paid taxes to the amount of $1,365,000, or 8 per cent. on the rental.

Thus, in Havana, a house valued at $10,000 will rent, it is estimated, for $800, and will pay a tax of about $70; in New York a property of the same value pays a tax two or three times as great. Last year the tax was 1 9-10 per cent.; a property of a friend of mine, which was valued at $10,000, was taxed at $191. This year the tax rate in New York is 2.14 per cent., and the same property will pay $214.

Another important factor in estimating the public wealth is represented by the mortgage operations, as these determine the territorial value which a country possesses only when it has reached a very advanced stage of progress. In the majority of the Latin-American countries the urban and rural real estate, outside of the capitals and principal ports, has hardly any value compared with the rent which it brings. In those countries very often a property which rents for $10,000, and represents a capital of from $100,000 to 150,000, if sold for cash would bring hardly a fifth of its value, and sometimes even less; the price must be made payable in instalments, and in that way, perhaps $40,000 or $50,000 may be obtained, to be paid in instalments of $10,000 yearly; that is to say, the same sum as the property would produce in rent in four or five years.

Cuba, owing to the present insurrection, is now in this situation in regard to her credit, which will not become stable again for many years to come. If the Island should separate from Spain the present generation will assuredly not see it so.

The value of the real estate sold in Cuba during the year 1894 was $18,000,000 in round numbers; that is to say that real estate was sold at an average of 91 per cent. on its nominal value; and if it be taken into account that in 1894, two years previously, the country had passed through an economic crisis, the result chiefly of the universal decline in the price of sugar, the basis of the wealth of the Island, it will be readily understoood that this difference was quite natural, and only shows that the value of property fluctuated then in Cuba in the same way as it would have done in any country in Europe or North America.

In the same year mortgages were paid off to the value of $3,677,000, distributed in 949 parcels; of these liquidations only forty-seven, or 5 per cent. of the total number, were of a legal character; that is to say, obligatory. In regard to the new loans made during the year, they reached a total of $3,875,000, or less than 1 per cent. of the full value of the property.

I think that the above data will suffice to give a correct idea of the social condition and the material prosperity of Cuba in 1895.

The only republic whose paper has been quoted at a premium is Chili, which, according to the statistics here given, shows a condition of credit and prosperity exceptional on the American continent, and if the paper of Cuba has also been at a premium I do not by any means imagine that this was because it was called "Cuba," but because it was a Spanish debt, for it must be borne in mind that all the Spanish public debts converted into one, consolidated in 1881, with coupons at 4 per cent. interest, payable quarterly, bear 6 per cent. interest from the date of consolidation and have never fluctuated more than three or four points, and that only momentarily, owing to speculations on the exchange. Just now, taking up the first Spanish newspaper at hand, and looking for the quotation of the debt I find: "Paris, 15 (of July), Foreign Spanish, 64.40."

In my opinion, if the Cuban insurrection had not occurred, Cuba would now owe $50,000,000 or $60,000,000, which would have been employed on such works of public utility—a central railroad, the irrigation of agricultural zones and the canalization of rivers, &c., as Spain has, and which in Cuba would perhaps have doubled the value of the public and private wealth.

The worst thing that could possibly befall Cuba would be that she should not have a debt, for without loans the development of her hitherto undeveloped resources would not be possible.

VII.

The Budget of the Island is no doubt exceedingly defective, and especially so in the branch of expenditures; this, however, has not been ruinous, for the country has been in a situation to pay its amount. In my opinion it might be and ought to be greater, with the difference that the expenses of the Department of Public Works and Instruction be increased, and the manner of collecting the revenues altered. But the new Law of Reforms passed in 1895 seeks to correct in part the faults of the Budget, which was chiefly defective from the injudicious manner of its distribution, for the Council of Administration of the Island in Havana, where it will be easier to attend to the wants of the country than from the Peninsula, is to arrange and vote the Budget in all that relates to the departments of public works, telegraphic and postal communication and means of transport by land and sea, to agriculture, industries and commerce, immigration, colonization and public instruction, charities and health.

The Budget of 1892–93 was $23,074,000; that of 1893–94 and 1994–95 increased to $26,000,000, without any increase, however, in the appropriation for works of public utility, to the decided discontent of the taxpayers.

With this last sum the amount per capita which the country was taxed was $15, Cuba thus occupying the seventh place among the Latin-American countries, for Cuba is not, as is so frequently asserted, the country most heavily taxed.

See the following table of taxation per capita:

	Per Capita.		Per Capita.
Chili,	$23	Argentina,	$16
Brazil,	22	Hayti,	16
Uruguay,	20	CUBA,	15
Costa Rica,	19		

Of these $15, $6.50 go to the payment of the interest on the public debt, which amounts to $10,500,000 annually. This sum does not benefit the country in any degree, as it is sent abroad for the payment of the coupons of the public debt.

Of the remainder, that is to say $15,500,000, more than $14,000,000 remain in the Island; of this amount, unfortunately, only a small part is expended on public works or on material; the remainder is expended on the salaries of the employees, but as living expenses in Cuba are greater than in any other country in the world, with the exception of the United States, and the employees, whether they be Cubans or Spaniards, cannot live on air, very few of them are able to save anything out of their salaries. Those who send money to Europe, or take money with them when they leave the Island, generally obtain it by speculations, not always honorable, perhaps, in which the Spanish and Cuban merchant alike take part, for neither is immaculate and they both want to make money.

The Budget of Revenues is derived from direct taxation, the revenues of the State and the customs; these represent 45 per cent. of the Budget.

The tariff is one of the sources of the public revenues which most requires a radical change. The duty on exports (although not more than three-fourths per cent. of the value of the products, according to the official appraisement, the articles being appraised on the basis of the minimum value, it affects them really only to the amount of one-half per cent.), is irritating and ought to be abolished, as it is abolished in the new tariff which is about to be laid before the present Cortes.

The duties on imports also require a radical change, for, while many superfluous or little used articles pay comparatively little, others, which are necessaries of life for the majority of the people, are excessively taxed. The tariff in general is as defective as those of the republics, although in these the system of taxation is more irregular and primitive.

In Uruguay, however, the tariff is more burdensome for the consumer, for while the average duty on imports is 30 per cent. of their value (in Cuba it is 25), many articles necessary for subsistence or for the development of the industries of the country pay, the former 50 per cent. and the latter 20 per cent. ad valorem. In Uruguay two-thirds of the amount of the Budget are derived from the customs. In Mexico, the majority of articles pay even more—60 per cent.; in Guatemala an average of 70 per cent., and so on in the majority of the sister countries.

The public debt amounted in 1894 to $170,000,000, that is, $100 per capita, being less than that of Uruguay, but as much as that of the Argentine Republic.

But this figure cannot justly be compared with that of other countries, since the Cuban debt was created altogether in consequence of the ten years' insurrection. The Cuban people, who in general took no part in the insurrection, and who now see that if its leaders had had more love for their country than desire to gratify personal ambition or personal animosities it would never have taken place, very naturally complain of having to bear so heavy a burden; but those who were the cause of that evil, as they are now of the new debt which is being created, should have the courage of their acts and be willing to bear all the consequences.

In any case, had the independence of the Island been

realized, in virtue of a treaty by which Cuba should recognize that debt, as was proposed, it would not be merely $10,000,000, which we are paying now—at 6 per cent. interest—but $13,000,000 or $14,000,000 that we should have to pay; and in case we did not pay it, which would have been very probable, as the wealth of the country would in all likelihood not have increased as it did from the peace of Zanjón down to 1895, the credit of Cuba would have declined to the level of that of some of the other countries which, through their failure to comply punctually with their foreign obligations, are continually engaged in conflicts with the governments of their creditors, and lead a mean and stationary existence, notwithstanding the great resources of their territories.

According to the "Report of the Council of Foreign Bondholders" of 1895, the amount of the debts of a number of republics that were neither amortixed nor gained interest, amounted to £71,675,000 sterling:

Argentine Republic,	£39,416,000	Costa Rica,	£2,050,000
Honduras,	15,622,000	Guatemala,	1,956,000
Venezuela,	7,498,000	Paraguay,	913,000
Colombia,	3,910,000	Nicaragua,	302,000

Compare with this the quotations of the principal Spanish-American bonds on the Paris Bourse on February 2 of last year:

	Per Cent.		Per Cent.
Of Cuba,	102½	Of Guatemala,	28
Chili,	102	Ecuador,	25
Mexico,	73⅝	Colombia,	15
Uruguay,	47	Paraguay,	12
Argentine Republic,	41	Honduras,	10
Costa Rica,	29		

VIII.

Owing to the increase in the cultivation of the agricultural products of Cuba, and especially of sugar and tobacco, within the last ten years, her commerce had attained proportions truly extraordinary. The country which has profited most by this agricultural development is the United States, and this it is perhaps which has awakened in a certain portion of the American people, which, it is to be said, however, is neither the largest nor the best, that desire to extend the territory of the Union to the Antillian Sea, which is the principal cause of the evils from which Cuba is to-day suffering.

From $90,000,000, to which the commercial movement amounted in 1880, it had risen in 1892 to $170,458,553, as follows:

Imports . . $69,444,287 | Exports . $101,014,266

The following table shows the increase as compared with that of the republics of the continent:

INCREASE IN TRADE IN TWELVE YEARS.

	1880-82.	1890-92.	Increase.
CUBA, . . .	$90,000,000	$170,000,000	$80,000,000
Argentine Republic, .	100,000,000	163,800,000	63,000,000
Brazil, ...	268,000,000	317,000,000	49,000,000
Chili, ...	99,000,000	131,100,000	32,100,000
Uruguay, ...	40,000,000	61,400,000	21,400,000
Mexico, ...	53,000,000	73,000,000	20,000,000
Porto Rico, ...	24,000,000	33,000,000	9,000,000
Guatemala, ...	8,100,000	14,400,000	6,300,000
Colombia, ...	28,000,000	33,900,000	5,900,000
Costa Rica, ...	6,500,000	11,700,000	5,200,000
Bolivia, ...	600,000	3,500,000	2,900,000
Santo Domingo, . .	3,400,000	6,300,000	2,900,000
Venezuela, ...	33,300,000	35,700,000	2,400,000
Paraguay, ...	3,300,000	5,600,000	2,300,000

In the remaining countries either the increase has been less, there has been none, or there has been a diminution.

Twelve years of peace sufficed to double the commercial movement of Cuba.

The value of the imports and the amount of their annual consumption per capita in the years of 1890–93 were as follows:

	Imports.	Per Capita.
Uruguay,	$32,364,000	$45.6
CUBA,	69,444,257	43.4
Chili,	65,090,000	26.6
Costa Rica,	5,423,000	22.3
Argentine Republic,	67,165,000	16.8
Brazil,	143,055,000	10.7
Paraguay,	2,744,000	8.5
Venezuela,	16,274,000	7.
Ecuador,	6,510,000	5.1
Colombia,	13,445,000	3.4
Guatemala,	5,010,000	3.3
Mexico,	28,000,000	2.4
Peru,	6,159,000	2.4

Total, $491,999,000, for a total population of 43,000,000, from which it follows that, while the inhabitants of the majority of the Spanish-American republics buy imported articles to the value of $11 per capita, in Cuba each inhabitant buys to the value of $43 annually.

Of these imports the following were from the United States:

	Per Cent.		Per Cent.
Mexico,	45	Peru,	32
Argentine Republic,	41	Ecuador,	11
CUBA,	29	Colombia,	9
Guatemala,	26	Brazil,	7
Venezuela,	25	Chili,	6
Costa Rica,	24	Uruguay,	3

or a total of $100,000,000 of which Cuba alone purchases one-fifth. In the year 1894, in consequence of the treaty of commerce concluded between Spain and the United States, Cuba consumed American products to the value of $33,617,000, or 52 per cent. of her imports.

The value of the exports in the principal South American republics and the proportion per capita, estimated in dollars, was as follows:

	Value of Exports.	Per Capita.
CUBA,	$101,000,000	$63.1
Uruguay,	29,000,000	41.
Costa Rica,	6,300,000	25.
Argentine Republic,	96,700,000	24.2
Chili,	66,000,000	23.5
Brazil,	174,000,000	12.5
Paraguay,	2,900,000	9.
Venezuela,	19,500,000	8.4
Guatemala,	9,400,000	6.2
Colombia,	20,400,000	5.
Ecuador,	6,400,000	5.
Mexico,	45,000,000	4.
Peru,	6,600,000	3.

The following table shows the total amount of foreign trade and the amount per capita in the several countries in 1892:

CUBA.

$106 per inhabitant.

Population, 1,600,000. Foreign trade, $170,000,000.

URUGUAY.

$83 per inhabitant.

Population, 700,000. Foreign trade, $61,000,000.

COSTA RICA.

$45 per inhabitant.

Population, 243,000. Foreign trade, $18,000,000.

CHILI.

$42 per inhabitant.

Population, $2,800,000. Foreign trade, $130,000,000.

BRAZIL.

$40 per inhabitant.

Population, 14,000,000. Foreign trade, $587,000,000.

HAYTI.

$35 per inhabitant.

Population, 572,000. Foreign trade, $20,000,000.

PORTO RICO.

$27 per inhabitant.

Population, 800,000. Foreign trade, $33,000,000.

VENEZUELA.

$19.50 per inhabitant.

Population, 2,300,000. Foreign trade, $36,000,000.

ARGENTINE REPUBLIC.

$15 per inhabitant.

Population, 4,000,000. Foreign trade, $242,000,000.
(Paper money.)

It is generally supposed that the only products of Cuba are sugar and tobacco. This is a serious mistake.

Some persons lay the blame for this deficiency of products on the Government, while very many enlightened people think that the spirit of indolence which prevails in the country is responsible for it.

In Cuba the habits of routine established in other countries have not yet become deeply rooted, because Cuba came only yesterday, as one might say, into commercial and political existence, and has no traditions, which, while they are of great value to a people from a social point of view, are often a hindrance to material progress.

Without counting cane sugar and tobacco, her exportations of other products would be sufficient to give Cuba a place among exporting countries. The other fruits and products exported by her represent a sum equal to, if not greater than, that of the foreign trade of many independent countries.

We give below the official statement of the exportation of different fruits, according to the annual record of the Chamber of Commerce of Havana, of 1892 (January 1), corresponding to the year 1891:

Mineral products, .	$1,700,000	Sweetmeats, . .	$130,000
Timber, . . .	842,000	Sweet Potatoes, Onions, &c., . . .	110,000
Bananas, . . .	700,000	Cattle, . . .	100,000
Pineapples, . .	450,000	Cocoanuts, . .	91,000
Coffee and Cacao, .	450,000	Oranges, . . .	58,000
Hides, . . .	310,000	Various other exports,	610,000
Wax and Honey, .	287,000		
Sponges, . . .	150,000		
		Total, . .	$5,988,000

In addition to these, rum and brandy were exported to the value of $1,000,000, and molasses to the value of $1,500,000, neither of which I have included, as they are products of the sugar cane.

These exports amount in value to $6,000,000, that is to say, about the same as those of Ecuador, which has almost the same population as Cuba; or as those of Bolivia and Santo Domingo, which together have twice as many inhabitants as Cuba.

In addition there are in the Island many factories, which manufacture goods not only for home consumption, but also for exportation to the neighboring countries.

IX.

To complete the picture which I have attempted to draw, comparing the condition, social and economic, of the Spanish Antilles and the Spanish-American Republics, it now remains to compare them in regard to their political condition and the liberities which they enjoy.

The policy pursued by Spain in Porto Rico and Cuba from 1836 to 1868 was most disastrous; owing to it the germ of independence brought from the continent and developed in the heat caused by the uncompromising policy of the Government, produced down to 1855, as hybrid fruits, a few isolated attempts at revolution, insignificant in themselves, but of importance because they alarmed the Spanish Government without, unfortunately, making it modify its policy of repression, but on the contrary causing it to carry out this policy still more stringently, thus increasing the causes for discontent which the country already had.

The advance in modern ideas which was made in Spain at that time also reached the Antilles, and when a radical change in the policy of Spain was about to be made it was also determined to modify the system of government in Cuba and Porto Rico conformably with the aspirations and the needs of the islands.

For this reason the thoughtful men of Cuba, the men of political weight, were then, as they are now, opposed to separation.

The revolution known in the history of Spain as the Revolution of September, which resulted in the exile of Isabella II. and the formation of a regency, with the Duke de la Torre at its head, under the guarantee for the people of an altogether democratic Constitution, with universal suffrage and other entirely liberal laws which gave the Spanish people a direct intervention in the government that it had not before had, would have given Cuba the same rights, had it not been that three weeks after the establishment of this government in Spain a revolution broke out in the Island, on October 10, of a separatist character, under the leadership, not of adventurers like the majority of the leaders of the present insurrection, but of ambitious and visionary young men, which, alarming the Government, placed the Island on a war footing and prevented for the time all change in the political situation.

The fact that when the Constitution was voted it was extended, with universal suffrage and the other civil and political laws of 1869, to the Island of Porto Rico, is the best proof that Cuba would have obtained the same liberties if the country had not been placed on a war footing.

Therefore it is that I have called that insurrection untimely. To wait thirty-two years in order to rebel against the mother country just at the moment when she was changing radically her political organization, for the purpose of obtaining liberties which up to that time Spain herself had not enjoyed, and which she was only then beginning to enjoy, was altogether unjustifiable.

A few months more of waiting and Cuba, too, would have had those liberties; so many lives would not have been uselessly sacrificed, nor would a debt of so many millions have been incurred.

This insurrection terminated, and I have already shown the advance which was effected by it in political evolution in Cuba, to the extent of causing the majority of the Peninsulars to adopt a decentralizing policy and to form a Liberal Reformist political party on the basis of administrative self-government.

With all these perturbations, and with all the defects of the system of government which it has had, I will now proceed to show—and this is the object of the present chapter—that in Cuba greater tranquillity and more political liberty have been enjoyed than are enjoyed in any of her sister countries ruled by themselves.

In the first place, in the majority of those countries the head of the State has been *almost always* a soldier, for it is rare to find a Spanish-American citizen of standing who does not possess a military title and who does not owe his position rather to his personal influence, employed in favor of or against the Government, than to his intellectual worth.

In Cuba also we have the misfortune to have a soldier at the head of the Government, but he is aided by a Secretary-General, who directs the political and civil administration of affairs, and who is generally a civilian ; it is true that he is not a Cuban; but, in exchange, the Cubans who belong to the administrative professions have as a field for the exercise of their abilities, in addition to our own country, Spain, Porto Rico and the Philippines; that is to say, several countries having a total population of 24,000,000.

If we pay without any benefit to the country $7,000,000 or $8,000,000 annually for the Departments of War and Marine, in those countries also large sums are annually spent (in the Argentine, $13,000,000 ; Venezuela,

$5,000,000, &c.), with the difference in our favor that while for us the army is only a costly European luxury, for those countries; besides being costly, it is also prejudicial, for it is the cause of the continual revolutions and disturbances in the midst of which the people live, and which are the principal, if not the sole reason, why those countries in general do not progress more, for they keep away capital, discredit them and produce distrust abroad, and serve some few as a ladder to climb to power or to obtain coveted positions.

We complain of our laws, although in reality they are in substance the same as the laws of those countries; for, except in questions of detail, they are all based on the spirit of the Roman law; and the later laws, which are more like regulations, are modeled on the obtrusive and parsimonious French law of Napoleon III., which we, too, had the misfortune to copy.

As for the application of the laws, if this is bad it is not because of the laws themselves, but because of the character of our people; and the only difference which I have observed between Cuba and her sister countries in this respect is that our authorities apply the law according to their own interpretation, if the injured party does not know how to assert his rights; while in those countries the authorities act according to their own caprice, without taking any account whatever of the law.

Many of those who have emigrated from the countries referred to for political reasons can testify to this fact, to which I myself have on more than one occasion called the attention of my American friends.

Both in Cuba and in Porto Rico, as a Cuban and a Spanish citizen I have publicly denounced the judicial acts of the authorities when I have thought them censurable; sometimes I have been prosecuted with the utmost rigor of the law, but the law itself has served to protect me and bring me out of the conflict victorious. In many of the

South American states, with popular institutions and other *nominal guarantees*, the citizens do not enjoy half as much liberty of speech and action as do those of Porto Rico and Cuba.

I will not cite examples, for by so doing I might wound the susceptibilities of those who are our brothers by origin, but I will point out some of the results of the political backwardness of many of those countries, which any observant person may perceive for himself.

The unbroken circle of civil wars, revolts and epochs of repression, of real reaction, in which political life revolves in those countries, has for its chief cause the inordinate desire for power of their public men, and the constant but never realized desire of the people to assert their rights, which disposes them to follow any ambitious leader who wishes to seize the supreme command or to attain whatever other aims he may have, without waiting for time or his own merits to justify his claims.

Thus those countries have for many years alternated between a weak and unstable government and a despotism.

Mexico, for example, previous to the rule of General Diaz, who, at the same time that he is a soldier, has proved himself an able statesman, had an infinity of military revolutions and changes of the fundamental laws of the state, although not so many as Ecuador, whose Constitution was altered in 1833, 1841, 1861, 1869, and 1883 successively.

In Mexico, in the space of thirty-one years there were thirty-six Presidents; between 1846 and 1847 not less than eight, and from 1857 to 1858, four. On the other hand, in a period of forty-one years only three men have held the supreme power. At least half of the Presidents have ruled provisionally.

In Venezuela the same thing has occurred; Paez ruled for twenty years, and Guzman Blanco seventeen; it being worthy of note that it was during these periods that the progress of the country was greatest.

Guatemala similarly had in twenty-five years nineteen Presidents, and three in a period of thirty-two years.

And if this has occurred in countries where the influence of an exotic race, hostile to the white race for historic and ethnic reasons, did not exist, let us consider for a moment what might occur in a country where a quarter of the population is irreconcilably hostile to the remainder, which, on the other hand, has not ceased to hold certain prejudices, justifiable to some extent, against the former.

X.

Of the present insurrection I shall say but little; it was brought about by the action of the separatist party in New York, aided by some young men in Cuba, visionaries whose convictions, neither very firm nor very profound, had no more solid foundation than a youthful spirit of adventure, exaggerated by the national temperament and the habit of judging the most serious questions, such as social and political questions are, without a previous study of them, considering results only without searching for their causes. These were joined, as the insurgent contingent, by a portion of the agricultural laborers, those who were by nature most inclined for the life required by the jungle; men of very simple habits, unused to the comforts of domestic life, and without attachment for the home; for neither in the Antilles nor on the South American continent does there exist among the proletarian class the ideal of the home as it is understood in Europe, or in the United States, by the same class.

A thorough understanding of the manner of life of the day laborer, and more especially of the mulatto and the negro, in those countries is indispensable in order to be able to estimate at its exact value an uprising of the character of the present insurrection.

In no country does the day laborer earn comparatively better wages than in Cuba—from $1 to $1.50 a day; and as the majority of the agricultural labors are performed by the job, if the laborer is industrious it is not unusual for him to earn $2 or $3 a day. He is very frugal in his habits, and with 40 cents a day he can provide for all his wants, smoking included. For clothing he requires only a pair of trousers, a shirt and a hat, which altogether cost perhaps $2, or even less. The rest of his earnings he spends in superfluities; but as he does not make himself the slave of these, whenever he wishes he can dispense with them without considering it a sacrifice; and in his house, which is constructed of wood and straw, and which consists of two rooms, one in which the women and the father of the family sleep, and another which serves as a parlor, dining room and pantry, and in which the sons and the friends of the family sleep, for the Cuban peasant's hospitality is such that in every rancho there is always some visitor to spend the night—some friend, old or new, who either lives in the house or who is staying for the night, after having dined with the family.

This custom of hospitality was not lost in Cuba even in the ten years' war through which the country passed. From the poorest hut to the richest mansion it is the general rule for the family to have some guest.

The hammock to sleep in, a table (which is not used for meals, however, for everyone eats with his plate in his hand, seated on a bench, on the floor, or in the hammock), and a few wooden benches with leather backs and seats, constitute the furniture; a wooden chest serves as a press, and in this everything they have—which is unhappily very little—is kept; the men usually have two suits of clothes, the one which they are wearing and another in the wash; two hats, one for every day, and a panama hat worth $16 or more—for this is his great luxury—for feast days. These and a pair of shoes, a pair of spurs and a good machete, in addition to the one used in his daily work, constitute the outfit of the unmarried peasant, and this apparel he carries tied up in a bandana handkerchief when he roams from place to place.

This, together with the facility with which he can find free lodgings everywhere, causes the "*guajiro*" insensibly to become detached from the home and to habituate himself to a semi-nomad life.

I have known in Matanzas, for instance, young men of twenty, from the Orient, who had been away from their homes for two or three years without having once visited them, who had traveled through the greater part of the Island and worked at every kind of agricultural occupation and every industry followed in it.

With this way of life, the Cuban being in general rash to temerity, and strong to bear the fatigues of traveling, and there being in the Island more than *five hundred thousand houses*, nearly 300,000 of them in the provinces of Santiago de Cuba, Puerto Principe and Las Villas, the fact is indeed in no way strange that the leaders of the insurrection should soon have found themselves at the head of numerous followers.

That the insurrection was not a spontaneous movement of the Cuban people was evident from the fact that neither the better portion of the population, the educated and intelligent classes, nor those who had given proof of real patriotism joined the insurrection; nor did any large part of the working classes join it when the insurgent bands scoured the country in search of recruits; not even those who were out of work and who, it might have been supposed, would join it in order to obtain a means of subsistence, for nine-tenths of the sugar cane crop being destroyed and the remaining crops abandoned, more than 150,000 men had been left without work.

The news that comes to us from the separatist camp clearly shows what kind of people they are who have swelled the insurgent ranks.

Setting aside the partiality of the source of the news, we see that those who have joined the insurgent camp are Cuban young men of good families who have lived for many years abroad; naturalized foreigners and men who, although not born in Cuba, call themselves Cubans and consider that they have the right to intervene in the history of the country because their families are of Cuban origin; men who, in reality, have very little knowledge of the social or political condition of the Island, but who cherish a peculiar affection for it founded on biased descriptions of its situation as it was thirty years ago.

Others are soldiers *by profession;* that is to say, men who, like the Scotch and Swiss in former times, hire their swords and fight for any cause, whether it appeals to their sympathies or not; others are actuated by even lower motives than this; individuals who have been obliged to expatriate themselves and who wish to forget some episode in their past lives in the fierce excitement of war; or men like those Italians who carry a hand-organ about the streets from morning till night, fancying that they are artists and are leading an independent existence *without having to work.*

Besides these foreign elements, who are those that have joined the insurrection? Adventurers who abandon civilization because they are obnoxious to it, like the so-called Captain Wilson, who headed a small expedition which landed last January on the eastern part of the Island, and who, as the American newspapers stated afterward, went to Cuba to avoid being compelled to appear before the Federal courts to answer a charge of having broken into and robbed a post office in Ohio.

Of the large number of men of weight and position who are in the Island very few, perhaps not 5 per cent., have gone over to the insurrection. Not one of all those whom I mentioned in a previous chapter has joined the insurgent ranks.

The men who still remain at home after a year of fighting, after the rebel bands have scoured the country and appeared in the neighborhood of every city—can they be considered as separatists at heart? I think not.

The Island has a rural population of more than 200,000 men who lived by agriculture or occupations connected with it; all these men possessed machetes and there were horses enough in the Island for all of them. When Maximo Gomez arrived in the Province of Havana in January last and marched to Pinar del Rio with Maceo, after having destroyed the crops of tobacco and sugar cane, what hope had these laborers of being able to earn a living? None.

Want spread through the Island; the wealth of the country was destroyed for the time being—for it is as easy to destroy as it is ridiculous to suppose that an army can defend what cannot be defended. In the times of the barbarian irruptions the people were pastoral; agriculture was not possible. In proportion as the peoples became civilized the cultivation of the ground extended, assuring the subsistence and the welfare of the people.

In spite of the method of warfare which the insurgents have pursued in Cuba, destroying its actual prosperity and well-being *in the name of the prosperity and liberty of Cuba*, which is the plainest proof that the leaders of the insurrection had nothing there to lose; that is to say, that they were foreigners in the country; those who had lost all or nearly all they had, and those who could lose nothing, because they had nothing to lose, allowed the wave to sweep over them and remained quiet; not even then did they join in the insurrection.

The revolutionists claim that they have 40,000 men under their flag; it is probable that the number is exaggerated, for, eager as they are to exaggerate everything concerning the revolution, it is not to be supposed that they would tell the truth in regard to a fact so important, morally and materially; but in any case, do 40,000 men (of whom only 8,000 or 10,000 are known to be engaged in any regular kind of warfare) form the majority in a country which has among its population 200,000 men of like conditions with those of the 40,000 mentioned?

And the few professional men and men of education who have joined the insurgents, are they of more weight than the numbers in the Island who for many years past have been laboring for their country's welfare?

The truth of the matter is that in Cuba the majority of the population, owing to the culture and enlightenment of the higher classes, and the prosperous condition of the lower, are opposed to war as a means of obtaining independence, for if the contrary were the case the insurgents would have not merely 30,000 or 40,000 men, but three or four times that number; it would be a general conflagration. The seat of government or capital of the republic would not at the present time need to be Cubitas, a mountain hamlet in the most solitary part of the least populous Province of Cuba.

The revolutionists who carry on the war from New York, in their eagerness to gain sympathizers outside of Cuba, constantly publish bulletins or fictitious telegrams and letters relating inhuman acts of the Spanish soldiers. "*The inhuman manner in which the war is carried on in Cuba.*" Which is folly, because war is human and peculiar to humanity. Other creatures have fights with each other at certain periods, but to kill one another at every period, as men have done since the world began, is peculiar to the human race.

War is barbarous, and as such it is natural that it should be cruel; to pretend that war shall be carried on and nobody shall be killed, or shall be killed *carefully and without being hurt*, is absurd. War is a terrible evil which can be terminated speedily only by heroic measures. And the only good thing there can be about a war is that it should terminate speedily.

In the Franco-Prussian war the Germans hunted the French peasants with the pretext that they were or might be sharpshooters. These, it is well known, did not wear a uniform in order that they might not be distinguishable from the peasants.

In the United States the Confederates treated their prisoners cruelly in Andersonville, Salisbury and Richmond. They slaughtered the garrison at Fort Pillow after it had surrendered. In the Southeast the butcheries of the guerillas of Quantrell are still remembered.

The Federals, on their side, have been accused of refusing for a long time to exchange prisoners for those who were subjected to the worst treatment in the Southern prisons; they burned Columbia, the beautiful capital of South Carolina, and also Atlanta. The march of General Sherman through Georgia was marked by the destruction of that region; they burned Richmond, and in the valley of the Shenandoah the devastation and destruction were complete. No one can forget the iniquitous proclamation of General Butler in New Orleans, ordering that the ladies who either by act or word should offer any insult to the Federal officers or soldiers should be treated as public women.

When men fight in war they become converted into wild beasts; the animal part dominates the intellectual, and it has but one object—to destroy.

For this reason war is to be avoided, and the war in Cuba was neither desired by the majority of the inhabitants nor necessitated by the aspirations for liberty of the Cuban people.

The majority of the people, in conjunction with the Autonomist party, labored for reform, and in a large measure successfully, as I have already shown.

As for the termination of the war, I now believe that it will not long be delayed, though, until very recently, I had grave doubts on this point, arising from the conviction founded on my intimate knowledge of the country, that the insurrection, like all other civil conflicts, could not be terminated by force of arms alone, or that if it could be so terminated it would be, for the time being, to the injury of Cuba, and therefore of Spain as well. To-day the attitude of the Spanish Liberal party in favor of the reforms and the declarations of the Conservative Government in Congress in regard to establishing them, at the same time that military operations will go on, make me cherish the hope that this strife between members of the same family will soon come to an end.

Señor Canovas recognizes the necessity of granting Cuba self-government, a decentralization so extreme as to give the country a large part of the administration of her own affairs, imposing on her the responsibility of the administration, and giving the public employments to native Cubans; a resolution which it is to be regretted the Government did not adopt last year while the illustrious General Martinez Campos was still in Cuba, to whom, indeed, much of the change which has taken place in Spain with respect to the manner of terminating the insurrection is undoubtedly due.

As a lover of my country, and of the honor of my ancestors, which is for me symbolized by that of Spain, I have labored for the cause of freedom in Cuba, rejecting, however, revolutionary methods that would not bring liberty to my country, but would, on the contrary, bring about a period of ruin and desolation, of reaction and exhaustion of the forces necessary to her progress, the end of which no one could foretell.

A sovereign state, unless it be great enough to make itself respected and to be able to maintain its rights abroad, has no guarantee whatever of liberty or peace; the latter, especially, will depend upon the interest or the convenience of the neighboring nations, if they are the stronger.

On the other hand, a colony with its own laws and with self-government, but under the sovereignty of a strong state, enjoys all the rights of a sovereign state and the credit and respect abroad which the mother country enjoys, and which in the colony becomes converted into a source of constantly increasing progress and well-being for its inhabitants.

www.ingramcontent.com/pod-product-compliance
Lightning Source LLC
Chambersburg PA
CBHW020552270326
41927CB00006B/811

* 9 7 8 3 7 4 4 7 2 8 8 5 0 *